King Arthur
and the
Grail Quest

King Arthur and the Grail Quest

—— ◆◆◆ ——

Myth and Vision from Celtic Times to the Present

JOHN MATTHEWS

Illustrated by
Steven Brown

BLANDFORD

To Richard (Kip) Carpenter

For Robin of Sherwood and perhaps for Arthur too!

First published in the UK 1995 by
Cassell plc
Wellington House
125 Strand, London WC2R 0BB

Previously published in hardback 1994
Reprinted 1995

Distributed in the United States by
Sterling Publishing Co., Inc.,
387 Park Avenue South, New York, NY 10016-8810

Distributed in Australia by
Capricorn Link (Australia) Pty Ltd
2/13 Carrington Road, Castle Hill, NSW 2154

British Library Cataloguing-in-Publication Data
A catalogue entry for this title is available from the British Library

ISBN 0-7137-2437-4 (Hardback)
ISBN 0-7137-2587-7 (Paperback)

Typeset by Method Limited, Epping, Essex

Printed and bound in Spain by Bookprint, S.L., Barcelona.

Frontispiece: *The Quest for the Grail*

Contents

Arthur riding the goat of
Capricorn, from the Zodiac
mosaic in Otranto, Italy

Introduction:
The Great Myths

UT OF THE MISTS THEY CAME: two great themes, two great stories, reflecting humanity's concerns with the sacred and the secular. Arthur, the hero of a dark time, assuming the mantle of a god; and the Grail, mystic object of quest and transformation. Their origins were both obscure – possibly unconnected – yet they seemed destined to be drawn together into a richly woven tapestry of myth, adventure, love and the desire for spiritual wholeness. Camelot and Corbenic; city and temple; knight and monk – from these seemingly irreconcilable elements came one of the greatest adventures of all time: the quest for the Grail. A quest which continues into the present and will continue for who knows how long yet as the future unfolds.

It seemed to me, when I began this book, that what was lacking was a good overall survey of the stories and how they had developed and become interrelated. What I have therefore attempted to do in these pages is to bring together the many strands of the two great themes, and to show how and when they changed and developed and what they grew into.

There are more than 100 extant texts which deal with the subjects of Arthur and the Grail. Many are still untranslated and are frequently obscure. To consider all of these texts, in the order of their appearance, is beyond the scope of this book; a select list will be found in the Appendix, with their approximate dates of composition. Extended summaries of these works, with occasional reference to others, will be given throughout the book, with the intention of making the complex history of the Grail and of Arthur as clear as possible to the general reader. For those who want a more detailed or scholarly approach, a full bibliography of both texts quoted and further reading will be found at the back of the book.

I have tried to deal with a selection of the best and most representative of these sources, which have been grouped as follows in the first four chapters (Chapter 5 deals primarily with the main themes in the Grail myth and how these have been carried forward into the present time):

Chapter 1   Nennius's *Historia Britonum*; Gildas's *De Excidio Britanniae*; The *Annales Cambriae*; Bede's *History of the English Church and People*; The *Dialogue of Arthur and the Porter*; 'The Stanzas of the Graves'; the poems of Taliesin

Chapter 2   *The Raid on the In-World*; *The Voyage of Bran*; The *'Elucidation'*; *Peredur*; *The Mabinogion*

Chapter 3   Geoffrey of Monmouth's *History of the Kings of Britain* and *Vita Merlini*; Chrétien de Troyes's *Perceval, or The Story of the Grail*; the chronicles of Wace and Layamon; the 'continuations' of *Perceval*

Chapter 4   *Vulgate Cycle*; Wolfram von Eschenbach's *Parzival*; *Perlesvaus*; Robert de Borron's *Joseph of Arimathea*; Sir Thomas Malory's *Morte D'Arthur*

Nothing can substitute for a reading of the texts themselves, and readers are encouraged to obtain these for themselves. The true magic of the Arthurian corpus lies within these great cycles of stories, written at a time when the world was still full of wonderment and the realms of Arthur and the Grail kings were seen as lying just beyond the next hill or in the next valley.

Here the knights rode in search of absolutes, and men and women came together in a quest which has continued to fascinate us through all the ages. Here was adventure, romance and mystery more than anyone could wish for. Lancelot, Gawain, Tristan, Iseult, Guinevere, Vivienne and Merlin – their names are a roll call of the great stories we read as children and which we still read today with reward and inspiration. Who can fail to be moved by the great vista of the central story – Arthur's mysterious birth, the founding of the Round Table, his marriage to Guinevere, the coming of Lancelot and the terrible ordeal of their love, the appearance of the Grail and the quest to discover its truth, which was to decimate the Fellowship of Knights and usher in the last dark days of Arthur's reign and his final mysterious departure to the Otherworld island of Avalon?

Many know the stories already, others know only fragments. In this book I have tried to fit together some of the pieces into a satisfactory whole. All that I have omitted, for reasons of space, awaits future publication and the reader's own quest for the Matter of Britain – as these stories are called by the men who wrote, listened to and read them.

These are the themes – sometimes mysterious, sometimes thrilling, always inspiring – which will occupy us in this book. Much is still tentative, still emerging from the twilight realm of the imagination where they were born. This is itself a quest, one which you may already have been following – as have I – for long years. So let us journey together for a while, sharing our insights and understandings of the search, marvelling at the wonders we may encounter, trembling at the terrors we may perceive, thrilling at the joys which are forever part of the quest.

JOHN MATTHEWS, *Oxford*

The Rise of Arthur: History and Myth in Early Britain

HEROES COME INTO BEING for a number of reasons. Sometimes it is a matter of putting right a wrong, as in the case of Indra or Robin Hood; sometimes it is to bring about a profound change in society, like Prometheus or Pandora; sometimes it is to extend the boundaries of the human soul; sometimes it is to quest for treasure, both in this world and in the other, like Jason's quest for the Golden Fleece. Arthur comes into being – the hero was born, as it were – to answer the call of a people with their backs to the wall.

THE BIRTH OF THE HERO

AT THE BEGINNING of the fifth century AD the once mighty empire of Rome was beginning to crumble. It would last for another few hundred years, but not as it had once appeared, stretching from Africa in the south to Scotland in the north, and from Spain in the west to Armenia in the east. Now its borders were shrinking back upon themselves; the legions began to withdraw, called home to protect the Eternal City itself.

In the far-off province of Britain, as the year 410 came to an end, the mists drew down again behind the last departing galley and the ancient land was once more returned to its previous masters, the Celts. Indeed, this fierce and independent people had never been truly subjugated and many areas of the island remained free of Roman influence.

Nor was the withdrawal all that sudden. In fact, as the historian Nora Chadwick remarks in her book *The Celtic Realms*: 'The Roman occupation of Britain can best be likened to a great flood tide, and the close came as the tide recedes, not by a sudden event, not even by a series of sudden events, but by a gradual process, as the ebb tide leaves the shore.'

Thus in 407 Constantine, the then governor of the province, was forced by the remaining legions in Britain to assume the title of Emperor and to lead an ill-fated exodus to Gaul. There he perished, though his name was remembered in Britain and we shall meet him again in a different guise later on. From this point onward, as the Byzantine historian Procopius declared: 'The Romans were never able to reconquer Britain, which continued to be governed by tyrants.' (Markale)

Yet nearly 500 years of Roman occupation had wrought their changes. The original network of native roads had been extended and improved, allowing greater freedom of travel and a wider system of commerce. The old scattering of trouble centres had been partially replaced by towns and cities which were largely self-governing after the manner of other Roman provinces. Many of the legionaries who had served in Britain chose to remain behind, having fallen in love with the soft hills and deep woodlands. Many had married native women and fathered families. Others had been granted tracts of land as payment for their military service and now scraped a living as farmers. Even the noble families of the native tribes had adopted Roman ways and were, in some cases, more Roman than their masters. A Romano-British aristocracy clung to its centres of power and tried to weld the tattered remnants of the Roman province into something like a whole.

Opposing them were a number of tribal leaders, the 'tyrants' mentioned by Procopius – petty kings ruling over a few hundred acres of land, raiding across the borders of their neighbours' land as they had done before the coming of the legions. Each one saw himself as a potential high king, receiving fealty from lesser lords, wielding supreme power in the land. Some of their names have survived amid the broken littoral of those dark days: Cunomagius, Vortiporix, and a greedy and ambitious man named Vortigern, who won many of the tribal leaders to his cause by promising that the legacy of Rome would be purged for ever from the earth of Britain. By whatever means, by 425 he had declared himself High King over all Britain, and by 450 most of the last vestiges of the old Roman system of government had broken down entirely.

During this time new enemies, as well as old, had appeared to harass the Britons. Picts and Scots from the north and Irish from across the sea to the west were raiding ever more deeply into the heartlands. Without the presence of the legions, there was little to prevent them, and now a new scourge, the Saxons, Angles and Fresians from Germany, began raiding all along the southern and eastern seaboards. To Vortigern is attributed the idea of setting one enemy against the other: offering lands to the Saxons in return for help in driving out the Picts and the Irish.

Three sources speak of this time, none judged reliable in all cases. The first is a work known as *De Excidio Britanniae*, attributed to a monk named

A map of Britain as it would have been in the time of the historical Arthur (fifth–sixth centuries)

AQUAE SULIS = Bath
CAERLEON ISCA = Caerleon on Usk
CAMULODUNUM = Colchester
CATRAETH = Catterick
CORINIUM = Cirencester
CORSTOPITUM = Cotbridge
DEVA = Chester
DIN EIDYN = Edinburgh
DUBRIS = Dover
EBURACUM = York
GLEVUM = Gloucester
ISCA DUMNONIORUM = Exeter
LINDUM = Lincoln
LUGUVALIUM = Carlisle
MÔN = Anglesey
SEGEDUNUM = Wallsend
SEGONTIUM = Caernarvon
VENTA = Caerwent
VENTA BELGARUM = Winchester
VIROCONIUM = Wroxeter

SCOTS

PICTS

Antonine Wall

Cambuslang

Din Eidyn

Coed Celyddon

Dumfriesshire • Arthur's Seat
Hadrian's Wall
Segedunum
Luguvalium   Corstopitum
Cair Ligualto
Catraeth
NORTH RHEGED   BERNICIA
Manau   Eburacum

SOUTH
RHEGED   DEIRA

Lindum
Môn
Segontium   • Deva   Baumber

GWYNEDD
MIDDLE
ANGLES   EAST
ANGLES
Viroconium

Caer Went   Camulodunum
Venta   Glevum
Corinium
Caerleon   Londinium
Isca   Aquae
Sulis
Brent   Wansdyke
Knoll   Badbury Hill
Beranburgh   Badbury   Venta Belgarum   Dubris
DUMNONIA   Cadbury   SOUTH SAXONS
Badbury
Isca   Rings
Dumnoniorum
Vecta Insula

Caer Guion

Gildas, which is really more of a diatribe against the evil tyrants – including Vortigern – who sought to restore the old pagan ways of the land and to outlaw the only recently established religion of Christianity.

Gildas's account of what happened next (laced with typical invective) is worth quoting in full:

> Then all the councillors, together with the proud tyrant Gurthigern [Vortigern], the British king, were so blinded that, as a protection to their country, they sealed its doom by inviting in among them (like wolves into the sheepfold), the fierce and impious Saxons, a race hateful both to God and men, to repel the invasions of the northern nations. Nothing was ever so pernicious to our country, nothing was ever so unlucky. What palpable darkness must have enveloped their minds – darkness desperate and cruel! Those very people whom, when absent, they dreaded more than death itself, were invited to reside, as one may say, under the selfsame roof. . . . A multitude of whelps came forth from under the lair of this barbaric lioness, in three cyuls, as they call them, that is, in three ships of war, with their sails wafted by the wind and with omens and prophecies favourable, for it was foretold by a certain sooth-sayer among them, that they should occupy the country to which they were sailing three hundred years, and a half of that time, a hundred and fifty years, should plunder and despoil the same.
>
> (Giles)

The second of these three sources, the *Historia Britonum* of Nennius, differs slightly from Gildas. Nennius, who probably lived towards the end of the ninth century, is somewhat more fanciful; he is making, in his own words, 'a heap of all he can find' putting together fragments from many sources.

> For years the Britons lived in fear. Vortigern was king of Britain and during his reign he was threatened both by the Picts and Scots. . . . Then three boatloads of men banished from Germany arrived. Among them were the brothers Hengist and Horsa, the son of Guietgils, the son of Guitta, the son of Wodin . . . the son of Geta, which made him son of god, not the God of gods, amen, the God of armies, but one of the idols they worshipped. Vortigern welcomed them and gave them the island they called Thanet, which the Britons call Rudhim . . .
>
> (Markale)

Once again Vortigern is the villain responsible for making the Saxons welcome, though here they are represented as men exiled, presumably for some unspecified crime.

The third and final source for this period comes from *A History of the English Church and People* by the Venerable Bede, written *c.* 731. His account reads as follows:

King Arthur of Britain by
Walter Crane

In the year of our Lord 449 . . . the Angles and Saxons came to Britain at
the invitation of King Vortigern in three longships and were granted
lands in the eastern part of the island on condition that they protected
the country: nevertheless their real intention was to attack it. At first
they engaged the enemy advancing from the North and having defeated
them, sent back news of their success to their homeland, adding that the
country was fertile and the Britons cowardly. Whereupon a larger fleet
came over with a great body of warriors, which, when joined to the original forces, constituted an invincible army. These also received grants of
land and money from the Britons, on condition that they maintained
the peace and security of the island against all enemies . . . These newcomers were from the three most formidable races of Germany, the
Saxons, Angles and Jutes . . .

Whichever of these conflicting versions one chooses to believe, the
effects were the same. More and more of the Saxons arrived in Britain,
hungry for lands and plunder. Nennius goes on to tell how Vortigern fell
for the charms of Hengist's daughter Rowena, whom he is said to have
married, and was persuaded to grant even larger tracts of land to his erst-
while 'allies'. Bede, taking the opportunity to attribute the causes of what
followed to the 'sins' of the Britons, continues:

It was not long before such hordes of these alien peoples crowded into the island that the natives who had invited them began to live in terror, for the Angles suddenly made an alliance with the Picts whom they had recently repelled, and prepared to turn their armies against their allies. They began by demanding a greater supply of provisions; then, seeking to provoke a quarrel, threatened that unless larger supplies were forth-coming, they would terminate their treaty and ravage the whole island. . . . In short, the fires kindled by the pagans proved to be God's just pun-ishment on the sins of the nation . . . these heathen conquerors devas-tated the surrounding cities and countryside, extended the conflagration from the eastern to the western shores without opposition, and estab-lished a stranglehold over nearly all the doomed island.

Bede goes on to paint a grim picture of cities burned to the ground, priests killed at their altars, wide-scale famine and death, people sold into slavery and whole communities put to the sword. Vortigern's standing, naturally, diminished rapidly from here on and he became a fugitive from his own people. However, his son, Guothermyr, raised an army and began fighting back against the Saxons – so successfully that he won several major victories against them. Then he died, possibly poisoned by the Saxons.

This temporary turnaround brought Vortigern back into favour suffi-ciently to enable him to attempt a conciliation with Hengist and Horsa. He arranged a meeting between his own chieftains, as many other British leaders as would still follow him and the Saxons. What followed is best told in the words of the redoubtable Nennius:

The enemy planned to overcome Vortigern and his army by cunning. . . . The Britons and the Saxons were to come unarmed to solemnly swear an alliance. But Hengist ordered his men to hide their knives [in their boots]. 'And when I say *Eu Saxones eniminit saxas*, take your knives out of your boots and attack them. But do not kill their king. For the sake of my daughter, his wife, take him prisoner because he will be more use to us as a hostage for ransom.' They promised to obey and went to the meeting. The Saxons spoke like friends and behaved with great courtesy. The men sat down so that each Saxon sat next to a Briton. Then Hengist cried out as he had said he would and the three hundred chiefs of Vortigern were all slaughtered. He alone was taken prisoner and put in chains. To save his life and win his freedom he had to cede many regions including Essex, Sussex and Middlesex.

This iniquitous event, afterwards known as the Night of the Long Knives, ended any support or respect that Vortigern possessed. He became a hunted man again, with every hand against him. Power now passed to a coalition of lords under the leadership of Ambrosius Aurelianus, who was

The Combat of the Dragons, Released by the Child Merlin from under Vortigern's Tower by Christian Loring

referred to as 'the last of the Romans', making it clear that he represented the faction who desired a return to Roman ways.

Ambrosius it was who sought, perhaps succeeded to some degree, to keep the spirit of the Roman civilization alive. He seems to have maintained something like a permanent military force, drawn from more than one tribe, to have kept the Roman roads open and to have offered some kind of defence for those who wanted only to pursue their lives in peace. He offered support and strength to the crumbling civil administration, which somehow continued to function for almost fifty more years.

Vortigern fled to Wales, where a few of his original followers still remained faithful. He was followed there, Nennius informs us, by Saint Germanus, who, according to some authorities, was Vortigern's natural son by his own sister. Whatever the truth of this, Saint Germanus seems to have had it in for Vortigern and to have carried out a furious campaign to discredit him and damn him still further in the eyes of the people. The end of the story is told by Nennius:

Vortigern fled in shame to the citadel of Guorthigern which is in the land of the Demetae near the River Tiebi. Saint Germanus followed him there also, and remained for three days and nights, fasting with his clerics. On the fourth night the whole fortress was set alight by fire from heaven . . . and Vortigern perished together with all his companions . . . Others again say that the earth opened and swallowed him up the night his fortress burnt around him, for after the fire nothing of him or his companions could be found.

Against this grim story of incest, betrayal and retribution, Ambrosius must have seemed like a veritable saviour. Under his leadership the Saxons were pinned down along the coastal regions and trade with the Continent was re-established. Oil, wine and Samian ware were imported by wealthy Britons, traces of which have been discovered all over Cornwall and Somerset. Sources generally imply that peace returned in some measure to the land at this time. As Bede puts it:

The Britons slowly began to take heart and recover their strength, emerging from the dens where they had hidden themselves, and joining in prayer that God might help them to avoid complete extermination. Their leader at this time was Ambrosius Aurelius, a modest man of Roman origin, who was the sole survivor of the catastrophe in which his royal parents had perished. Under his leadership the Britons took up arms, challenged their conquerors to battle, and with God's help inflicted . . . defeat upon them. Thence forward victory swung first to one side, and then to the other, until the battle of Badon Hill, when the Britons made a considerable slaughter of the invaders . . .

Mention of this battle is crucial, for it signals the appearance of a hero whose star was to rise rapidly to the ascendant, remaining there, almost unopposed, ever since. Heroes appear when they are most needed, and even with the presence of Ambrosius the new peace was a fragile thing. Saxons in the south and east and Picts in the north threatened upon three sides. The Britons needed a more virile focus for their new-found independence. Arthur provided that focus, and in so doing not only changed the face of British history but also established himself as one of its greatest and most enduring figures. It is Arthur, not Ambrosius, who is the victor of Badon.

THE COMING OF THE KING

IN TWO of the three sources we have been examining there is no mention of Arthur by name, though his presence can be inferred. Gildas, whose *De Excidio Britanniae* was written *c.* 540, claims to have been born in the year that the battle of Badon was fought, which makes him more or less contemporary with Arthur. Bede likewise mentions the battle, but without

Arthur Claims Excalibur by H. J. Ford. When Arthur needed a sword Merlin led him to a lake where a mysterious arm emerged from the water, holding the great weapon Excalibur, which Arthur made his own

naming the hero who led the Britons to a crashing victory against the Saxons.

Bede's interest was purely ecclesiastical and he may be forgiven for omitting Arthur's name and role. Gildas's silence is easily accounted for: his brothers were all pirates, and Arthur was responsible for capturing and executing them all. According to one account, when Gildas heard this he took the books in which he had recorded the history of the Arthurian era and, like Prospero, drowned them in the sea.

With these two sources excluded we are left only with our old friend Nennius and a rather doubtful document known as the *Annales Cambriae* (*Annals of Wales*), which, under the entry for 516, lists 'the battle of Badon, in which Arthur bore the cross of our lord Jesus Christ on his shoulders for three nights and the Britons were victorious' (Morris, 1980). This is clear enough in its reference to Arthur, but still does not tell us with any certainty that he was the leader of the Britons. For this we have to turn to a famous passage in which Nennius lists not one great battle but twelve:

At that time huge numbers of Saxons were invading Britain and increasing. When Hengist died, his son Octha came from North Britain to the kingdoms of the Canti and founded the royal line of Kent. Then Arthur and the British kings fought the Saxons. He was their *dux bellorum*. First he fought a battle at the mouth of the River Glein. He fought four others, on the River Dubglas in the region of Linnus. The sixth battle took place on the river called Bassas. The seventh was in the forest of Celidon, the *Cat Coit Celidon*. The eighth was the battle in the fort of Guinnion, in which Arthur bore the image of the Virgin on his shoulders. The pagans were put to flight that day and many of them were slaughtered, thanks to our lord Jesus Christ and the Blessed Virgin. A ninth battle took place at the City of Legions, a tenth on the banks of the River Tribuit. The eleventh on a mountain called Agned or Cat Bregouin. The twelfth battle took place at Mount Badon, in which a single assault from Arthur killed 960 men and no other took part in this massacre. And in all these battles he was victor.

This list has given more trouble to would-be chroniclers of the Arthurian period than almost any other. The names are unfamiliar, and their identification cannot be proven beyond a doubt. None the less they clearly establish Arthur as a foremost warrior, a *dux bellorum* or Duke of Battles, which makes him almost certainly a military leader rather than a king (this title comes much later, in the eleventh century, when the pseudo-historians and romancers turned Arthur into the noble and splendid king with whom we are still most familiar). The statement that Arthur slew 960 men single-handed has led many historians to dismiss Nennius's account as spurious, yet it need mean no more than that Arthur's own personal troops led the attack and were supremely successful.

As to the battles, the historian Nikolai Tolstoy has summarized the best guess of contemporary scholarship as to their probable placing.

The battle of Glein probably took place at or near the River Glen in Northumberland. It was fought against a force of Fresians under the command of Octha, Hengist's son.

The second, third, fourth and fifth battles were probably fought against Scots from Ulster (Dalraidia). Nennius places them on or close to the River Dubglas in the county of Lindsay. Tolstoy suggests the River Douglas, which is only three miles from the area known as Lennox (Linnius in Latin). Members of the Campbell family in that area claim descent from an Arthur ic Uibar, strengthening this supposition.

Battle number six, on the River Bassus, is placed at Cambuslang, long believed to be the burial place of a Pictish chieftain named Caw. Though the name Bassus has not been satisfactorily traced, Cam*bus*lang derives from *camus long*, 'the blight of ships', suggesting a possible seagoing engagement. According to more than one genealogy, the apoplectic Gildas was Caw's son, while his daughter Cwyllog may have been the wife of Medrawt, Arthur's nephew/son and his bitterest foe. There are clear references here to a lost story concerning some kind of feud between the families of Caw and Arthur; it is almost certainly the reason why there is no mention of Arthur in Gildas's work. If Tolstoy is correct in supposing this

Glastonbury: Pomparls Bridge and the River Brue, where local legend tells that Excalibur was returned to the waters (*John Rogers*)

battle was a seagoing engagement, it may even have been the one in which Gildas's piratical brothers met their end.

The seventh battle, at Cat Coit Caledon, has long been recognized as being fought in the areas once occupied by the ancient Caledonian forest. Tolstoy has narrowed this down even further by placing the battle at the meeting place of the borders between Peebles, Lanark and Dumfries. A Roman road crosses the mountains here, making this a good place for a skirmish. The enemy may have been a colony of Saxons from Dumfriesshire.

The eighth battle, at Guinnion, is tentatively identified with Caerguidn (Land's End) and seems to have been fought against a Saxon leader named Cerdic around the year 500.

The ninth battle, said to have been fought at the City of the Legions, is difficult to identify because there were several places which bore this name in Arthur's day. Chester was held to be the strongest contender and this still seems the most likely, though Tolstoy prefers Exeter, known by the Romans as Isca Dumnoniorum and by the Britons as Caer Wisc. Evidence from a thirteenth-century Welsh poem in the *Black Book of Carmarthen* suggests this was a battle fought either at sea or around a harbour. The hero Geraint, who fell in this battle, was from Devon; the haven at Exmouth therefore seems a distinct possibility.

Sir Richard Grenville's 1583 plan of Tintagel Castle and Island: this site has for long been associated with Arthur's birthplace, though there is in fact little evidence to support the claim. 1 'a cave'; 2 'the chapel'; 3 'a garden walled'; 4 'a fayer sprynge of water'; 5 'a place to land at; 6 'A, B, 2 Rampiers to defend the landing'; 7 'the wailles of the Iron Gate'

The tenth and eleventh battles respectively were said to have been fought at the River Tribuit or Tryfrwyd and Mount Agned, and for these Tolstoy suggests Brent Knoll for the hill and the nearby area of sands known as either Serts Flats or Berrow Flats as sites for a long and hard-fought encounter which was really a single battle rather than two.

All of these are important battles, and established Arthur as not only a redoubtable leader but also the commander of an extremely mobile force. This led the distinguished historian R. G. Collingwood to put forward the theory that Arthur led a force of mounted *cataphracti* – armoured cavalry of a type used both in Rome and Byzantium. This would have given Arthur the mobility and strength necessary to achieve the remarkable reversal of British fortunes which attended his great campaigns.

But it is the twelfth and final battle which sets Arthur's star at its zenith. This battle, before all others, smashed the Saxon forces and left them so

shaken that it was forty years before they dared attack in force again, by which time they were settlers rather than invaders, marrying into British families and establishing a stock which would eventually become a new race – the Anglo-Saxons.

In all probability, without Arthur none of this would have happened. The Saxons would have overrun Britain just as the Romans had done centuries earlier. As it was, something like a permanent peace was established which lasted until Arthur's death or disappearance *c.* 555.

Badon itself has been variously identified with Barham Down, Badbury Rings and Liddington Castle. The medieval pseudo-historian Geoffrey of Monmouth, who did more than anyone before or since to establish Arthur in the forefront of history, sets it as Bath in Somerset. Tolstoy, following this, suggests that Bathampton, which lies just outside the present city, fits the bill. He dates the battle to 501, though a slightly later date of 515 seems to fit the meagre shreds of information found in Gildas, Nennius and Bede.

This is almost the end of the story. For its close we must turn to the pages of the *Annales Cambriae*, which starkly portray the period in a few enigmatic lines. Under the year 537 we find the following entry: 'The Battle of Camlann, in which Arthur and Medraut fell; and there was death in Britain and Ireland.'

This is all that history has to tell of the passing of one of its greatest heroes. Later, much will be made of this. Medraut will become Mordred,

Arthur's bastard son (possibly by his own half-sister) and the two will become mortal enemies. Here we are told only that both fell, not that they were adversaries, or related. It is typical of the way that fragments of documented fact, eked out with oral tradition, augmented by imagination and the need for a hero of supernatural power, grow with the telling into the vast and wondrous edifice of medieval story. Ultimately Arthur's identity remains mysterious. In the pages of these chronicles, nearest to him in time, he appears and disappears without preamble or comment. He is simply there, does the work allotted to him and then, just as suddenly, vanishes. From this mystery spring many more. Arthur acquires a wonderful following of warriors, many as colourful and enduring as himself. His legend begins to grow – as it continues to do today – adding ever more extraordinary and amazing details. For the origin of some of these details we must look back to the days not long after his departure from this life, and perhaps even earlier, to the times before him. For there are two Arthurs – at least. We have seen something of the historical figure. Now it is time to look at the figure who stands behind him – the Arthur of myth.

THE MYTHIC HERO

ALTHOUGH THERE ARE comparatively few references to Arthur in either historical or pseudo-historical documents, there is another source which is rich – if sometimes obscure – in details of a very different and far larger figure. This source is the mythology of the Celtic peoples, especially of Wales and Cornwall. Here we find clues, hints and stories of rich and extraordinary texture, from which emerges a second Arthur.

As with all documents relating to myth and legend, it is hard to point to a date which might be considered the 'earliest' mention of Arthur. This is partly because the stories, poems and brief references were often not written down until after they had been circulating for several centuries in oral tradition. This is the case with a poem attributed to the sixth-century bard Taliesin, which may well be the first reference still extant not only to Arthur himself but also to his quest for a mysterious wonder-working object.

The *Preiddeu Annwn* or *Spoils of the In-World* (J. Matthews, 1990h) probably dates from the ninth century, some 400 years after the death of the historical Arthur, yet the references contained within it almost certainly refer back to a much earlier time – possibly even before the era of Arthur the *dux*. It tells the story of a voyage, in the ship *Prydwen*, to the Otherworld kingdom of Annwn, to steal a cauldron possessed of magical properties. We shall examine this story in more detail in the next chapter. For now it is sufficient to note that the poem places Arthur in both a heroic and a

Arthur

mythic mode of being, and that his presence in an Otherworldly setting is taken for granted.

Elsewhere, in the poems contained within *The Black Book of Carmarthen*, which was not actually compiled until the thirteenth century, are other references to Arthur which again suggest that he was a familiar figure in the repertoire of traditional poets and story-tellers. In a poem entitled 'The Battle of Llongborth', we read:

> At Llongborth I saw Arthur's men
> brave – hewing with steel –
> the Emperor's men, the Director of Toil.

This is not the only place where the term *Ameradfawr* (Emperor) is used of Arthur. He appears as such again in several extant poems from this early period. In one, a series of gnomic verses called 'The Stanzas of the Graves' which lists the last resting places of a huge gallery of heroes, we read:

> A Grave for March, a grave for Gwythur,
> A grave for Gwgawn Red-Sword –
> A wonder of the World is Arthur's Grave.
>> (Jones)

The last line is sometimes translated

> Not wise [the thought] a grave for Arthur

which has been taken to refer to the fact that Arthur was not dead and therefore one should not think of him as having a grave at all. If the first translation is accepted, it probably links Arthur to a number of wondrous graves mentioned elsewhere which have strange phenomena attached to them.

Another reference, in a poem attributed to Taliesin, mentions:

> The third profound song of the sage,
> Is to praise Arthur, Arthur the blest,
> With harmonious art:
> Arthur the defender in battle,
> The trampler of nine enemies.
>> (J. Matthews, 1990h)

But by far the most interesting of these early poems is a fragment, again found in *The Black Book of Carmarthen*, which is usually given the title 'Par Gur?' or 'What man?', from the opening line. I give the poem in full here because of the fascinating glimpse it offers into the world of early Welsh epic poetry and of the Arthurian story in particular. It is set in the form of a dialogue between Arthur himself and a porter or gatekeeper.

The Dialogue of Arthur and the Porter

'What man is the porter?'
'Glewlwyd Mighty-Grasp,
What man asks it?'
'Arthur and Cai the Fair'
'What company is with you?'
'The best in the world.'
'They shall not enter here
Unless you praise them.'
'I shall praise them,
You shall see them –
The Vultures of Elei –
The three great magicians:
Mabon Son of Modron,
Uther Pendragon's servant,
Cystaint son of Banon,
And Gwyn Goddyfrion.
Strong servants all
Defending the laws:
Manawydan son of Llyr
Great in council;
(Manawyd returned
With a broken shield
From Tryfrwyd)
And Mabon son of Mellt,
Who stained the grass with
    blood;
And Anwas the Winged,
And Llwch Llawynnawc
Who were each determined
To defend Dun Eidyn.
A lord would give them refuge,
Would even avenge them,
Cai would plead for them,
Even as he struck three at a
    time!
(When Celli was lost
Fury ranged free.)
Cai would plead for them
Even as he cut them down.
Though Arthur was laughing
He made blood to flow
In Afarnach's hall,
Fighting the hag.

He slew Pen-Palach
In the house of Disethach
On Eidy's Mount;
He fought the dogheads,
Felled them by the
    hundred –
By the hundred they fell
To Bedwyr the hewer.
On the shores of Tryfrwyd
In battle with the dog-man,
Furious his mien
With sword and shield.
Vain to compare
Even a host,
To such as he.
A sword in battle,
A giver of pledges,
A constant chief
To the host
Defending the land.
Bedwyr son of Rhyddlaw
With nine hundred listening
And six hundred attacking
Was well worth watching.
(I once had young men,
    followers,
It was better when they
    still lived.)
Before Lord Emrys [Ambrosius]
I saw Cai in a hurry
Leading the host,
Long in wrath,
Heavy in vengeance,
Terrible in battle.
When he drank from his horn,
It was enough for four men;
When he came into battle,
He slew enough for a hundred.
Unless God achieved it
Cai could never be slain,
Cai the Fair and Llachue,
Brave in battle,
Finished the fight.

On top of Ystawingun
Cai slew nine hags,
He went to Mon
To fight great cats.
He set his shield
Against Cath Paluc.
When people ask
"Who slew Cath Paluc?"
The answer shall be
That where nine score
    champions
And nine score leaders [failed,
Cai the fair did not].'

Despite the fragmentary and sometimes oblique nature of this poem (I have completed the last two lines from the sense of what goes before), it gives a powerful sense of the tough, bloody-handed battlers in Arthur's heroic band. Several of the heroes mentioned are familiar to readers of the later, medieval epics. This Cai, who fights the giant Cath Paluc, is better known as the acid-tongued blusterer Sir Kay, while Bedwyr becomes Sir Bedivere, Arthur's butler, charged with returning the magical sword Excalibur to the lake from where it came after Arthur's wounding at the battle of Camlann. Llwch Llawynnawc may well be the original Sir Lancelot.

The way in which Arthur and his followers were perceived, only a few generations after their passing, is well illustrated in the stories contained in the collection of Welsh mythology and legend known as *The Mabinogion* (Guest). This contains in all five stores set in and around the Arthurian court. Three of these, 'Geraint mab Erbin', 'Peredur son of Evrawc' and 'Owein', are closely related to later medieval stories and will be dealt with in the appropriate chapters; the others, 'Culhwch and Olwen' and 'The Dream of Rhonabwy', add further to the picture of the heroic Arthurian cycle.

None of the stories contained in *The Mabinogion* was written down until the thirteenth or fourteenth century, but these latter two in particular contain material which dates from much earlier. Both show signs of being composed no later than the ninth century, and were almost certainly circulating in oral tradition long before that – possibly even soon after the end of the actual Arthurian era. 'Culhwch' tells the story of the trials and tests undergone by the young hero to win the hand of Olwen, the daughter of the vast and uncouth giant Ysbaddaden Pencawr, who, when he is approached, threatens death to all-comers unless they undergo a series of tests, including the discovery of several mysterious objects: the Oxen of Glwlwyd, the Cup of Llwyr son of Llwyryon, the Hamper of Gwyddno Garanhir, the Harp of Teirtu, the Sword of Wrnach the Giant, and the comb and shears hidden between the ears of the great boar Twrch Trwyth.

According to tradition, Glastonbury was the site of the earliest Christian church (here shown as a suggested reconstruction, from Sir Henry Spelman's *Consilia*, 1664), founded by Joseph of Arimathea to house the Grail itself

The Court of Camelot, from a
nineteenth-century
engraving

To complete the tasks, Culhwch sets out for the court of Arthur – who is
his cousin in this tale – to enlist the aid of various heroes. In fact, not all of
the tasks described above are carried out in the ensuing story, but enough
clues are given to suggest a once substantial cycle of tales, featuring Arthur
and his heroes. The extent of this epic collection (for the most part lost to
us) is suggested by the immense list of the 250 heroes which takes up
several pages of the text. Each one has a striking or unusual epithet, suggesting his unique skill or ability. For example:

Sol, Gwadyn Ossol, and Gwadyn Odyeith (Sol could stand all day upon
one foot). Gwadyn Ossol, if he stood upon the top of the highest mountain of the world, it would become a level plain under his feet. Gwadyn
Odyeith, the soles of his feet emitted sparks of fire when they struck
upon things hard, like the heated mass when drawn out of the forge. He
cleared the way for Arthur when he came to any blockage.

(Guest)

At one time, we may presume, there was a story belonging to each of these curious individuals. We can only guess at the nature of these, but 'Culhwch' itself gives us a strong impression. The story is not only dramatic and full of magical events, it is also fast-paced and funny, and contains some of the most richly textured descriptions to be found anywhere in Celtic literature. For example, there is the justly famed description of Culhwch himself, as he first appears, setting out for Arthur's court:

And the youth pricked forth upon a steed with head dappled grey, of four winters old, firm of limb, with shell-formed hooves, having a bridle of linked gold on his head, and upon him a saddle of costly gold. And in the youth's hand were two spears of silver, sharp, well tempered, headed with steel . . . a gold-hilted sword was upon his thigh, the blade of which was gold . . . before him were two brindled white-breasted greyhounds, having strong collars of rubies about their necks, reaching from the shoulder to the ear. And the one that was on the left side, bounded across to the right side, and the one of the right to the left, and like to sea-swallows sported about him. And his courser cast up four sods with his four hooves, like four swallows in the air about his head, now above, now below. About him was a four-corner cloth of purple, and an apple of gold was at each corner, and every one of the apples was of the value of an hundred kine. And there was precious gold of the value of three hundred kine upon his shoes and upon his stirrups, from his knee to the top of his toe. And the blade of grass bent not beneath him, so light was his courser's tread, as he journeyed towards the gate of Arthur's palace.

(Guest)

If we consider that at one time bards travelled the land telling such stories, we cannot help but be impressed at the marvellous richness of such descriptive episodes, or the sheer mastery of detail which decorates the tale.

The Hero Sets Out by Huszti Horvath

The Gunderstrup Cauldron: this great work of Celtic art, discovered in a Danish bog, holds the key to much of the lost symbolism of the Celtic peoples; it is also one of the earliest images of the sacred vessel

Culhwch's quest to acquire the miraculous objects demanded by Ysbaddaden becomes an excuse for a riotous assembly of story fragments, woven by a master story-teller into a unique fabric. The centrepiece of the work is the great hunt for the giant boar Twrch Trwyth, which is graphically described as follows:

> And Mabon the son of Modron, came up with him at the Severn . . . and Arthur fell upon him together with the champions of Britain Osla Cyllellvawr drew near and Manawyddan the son of Llyr, and Cacmwri the servant of Arthur, and Gwyngelli, and they seized hold of him, catching him first by his feet, and plunged him in the Severn so that it overwhelmed him. On the one side, Mabon the son of Modron spurred his steed and snatched his razor from him, and Cyledyr Wyllt came up with him on the other side, upon another steed, in the Severn, and took from him the scissors. But before they could obtain the comb, he had regained the ground with his feet and from the moment that he reached the shore, neither dog, nor man, nor horse could overtake him until he came to Cornwall. . . . Then Arthur and his hosts proceeded until they overtook the boar in Cornwall, and the trouble that they had met with before was mere play to what they encountered in seeking the comb. But from one difficulty to another, the comb was at length obtained, and then he was hunted from Cornwall, and driven straight forward into the sea. And thenceforth it was never known whither he went . . .
>
> (Guest)

A Celtic warrior from the Gunderstrup Cauldron

In the end, of course, with a little help from the fair Olwen herself, the tasks are carried out and Ysbaddaden killed. Culhwch inherits his father-in-law's castle and treasure, and married his daughter in true faery-tale tradition. In the process we are treated to an array of wondrous events,

This image from the Gunderstrup Cauldron refers to the story of the magical vessel of renewal in which dead warriors were dipped, and from which they emerged alive again, but dumb

adventures and characters, which do more than hint at the richness of Celtic story, and make it plain that Arthur had become the centrepiece of a far older mythology, taking his place centre-stage as the prime mover in an already established cycle of native hero-tales.

There are even hints at a still older figure, whom we may call Arth, the Bear. Echoes of this being, perhaps even a god in his own right, still come down to us through the pages of the oldest Welsh texts. It may indeed be that the Arthur of history subsumed this earlier individual and acquired some of his larger-than-life characteristics. Certainly this is born out in the second of the older stories contained in *The Mabinogion*.

'The Dream of Rhonabwy' is really a story within a story. The hero, Rhonabwy, who may possibly have been a real person, is fleeing from his enemies and takes shelter in the hut of an ancient *gwrach* or hag. She allows him to sleep on a yellow oxhide, which induces a dream. In this he first of all encounters a huge warrior named Iddawg, who turns out to be one of Arthur's men. He takes Rhonabwy to Arthur's camp, where the warriors are preparing to fight the battle of Badon against Osla Big-Knife. There then follows a series of episodes which Rhonabwy witnesses, including a curious game of *gwyddbwyll* (similar to chess) between Arthur and his nephew Owein, which is constantly interrupted by messengers who bring news of a battle taking place in an adjacent field between Arthur's men and Owein's 'ravens' (we are not told but are led to assume that these are men who can take the form of ravens).

Celtic warrior from a bronze statue found at Volubilis in Morocco

Despite this, the game continues, so that it becomes a kind of symbolic representation of the actual warfare being enacted nearby. The story goes on:

So they finished [one] game and began another; and as they were finishing the game, lo, they heard a great tumult and a clamour of armed men, and a croaking of ravens, and a flapping of wings in the air, as they flung down the armour entire to the ground, and the men and horses piecemeal. Then they saw coming a knight on a lofty-headed piebald horse . . . and he told him [Arthur] that the Ravens had slain his household and the sons of the chief men of the island, and he besought him to cause Owein to forbid his Ravens. And Arthur besought Owein to forbid them. Then Arthur took the golden chess-men that were upon the board, and crushed them until they became as dust. Then Owein ordered Gwres the son of Rhegwed to lower his banner. So it was lowered, and all was peace.

(Guest)

THE SPLENDID QUEEN

AS WELL AS THE HEROES who constellate around the figure of Arthur, there is one other character in the story whose role is substantial. This is Guinevere, Arthur's queen. In the later, medieval sources she is a familiar figure – beautiful but ultimately betraying her husband with the romantic Lancelot. In the earlier, heroic texts a somewhat different figure emerges.

There are several mentions of Guinevere in Celtic literature. In the Welsh *Triads* we find her listed among the unfaithful wives of the Island of Britain:

One was more faithless than those three: Gwenhywfar,
Arthur's wife, since she shamed a better man than any
of the others.

Elsewhere in the same collection we hear of a triple Guinevere:

Three Great Queens of Arthur's court:
Gwenhywfar daughter of Cywryd Gwent,
and Gwenhywfar daughter of Gwythr ap Greidawl,
and Gwenhywfar daughter of Gogfran the Giant.

(Bromwich)

All these names are obscure, and it is unclear whether any one of the three is to be identified with the Queen. However, the last name is remembered in a popular Welsh rhyme which says: 'Gwenhywfar, daughter of

The omphalos, or central point, of Ireland, an early image of the Grail as stone, a theme reflected in Wolfram von Eschenbach's medieval poem *Parzival*

Ogfran the Giant – bad when little, worse when big.' In later, medieval tradition we are told of two Guineveres, twins but with different mothers, who are called the 'true' and 'false' Guinevere.

By far the clearest reference – and probably the earliest – appears in the *Vita Sanctae Gildae (Life of Gildas)* by the monk Caradoc of Llancarven. He substantially elevates the life of the saint until we would be hard put to recognize the irascible author of the *De Excidio Britanniae*. Here we read how Gildas arrived at Glastonia (Glastonbury) 'at the time when King Melwas was reigning in the Summer Country', and was well received. However, Glastonia

was beseiged by the tyrant Arthur with a countless multitude on account of his wife Gwenhywfar, whom the aforesaid wicked king had violated and carried off, and brought there for protection, owing to the asylum afforded by the invulnerable position due to the fortifications of thickets of reed, river, and marsh. The rebellious king had searched for the queen throughout the course of one year, and at last heard that she remained there. Thereupon he roused the armies of the whole of Cornubia and Dibneria; war was prepared between the enemies.

When he saw this, the abbot of Glastonia, attended by the clergy and Gildas the Wise, stepped in between the contending armies, and in a peaceable manner advised his king, Melwas, to restore the ravished lady. Accordingly, she who was to be restored, was restored in peace and good will.

(Williams)

This has a ring of truth about it. Or, at least, it sounds like a memory of events which may actually have taken place – though it is unlikely, in the light of what we know of Gildas, that he would have taken the trouble to intervene in any matter concerning 'the tyrant' Arthur!

The theme of Guinevere's abduction, however, echoes throughout Arthurian literature ever after. It is repeated by Geoffrey of Monmouth in his pseudo-history of Britain, and again in Malory's *Morte D'Arthur*, where Melwas reappears as Meleagraunce and Guinevere is rescued, not by Arthur, but by Lancelot. In mythological terms the story is one of several such abduction tales which refer to the ancient theme of 'the rape of the Flower Bride', in which the sovereignty of the land is represented by a woman whom the would-be king or ruler must win either in combat against an adversary or by marriage. In the case of Guinevere, Arthur's marriage to her signifies his partnership with the land; when the Queen is stolen away by Melwas, Arthur must win her back or lose his crown.

Behind this may well lie the seeds of the whole complex of stories relating to the illicit love of Lancelot and Guinevere. Seen through the eyes of the medieval romancers, this was a far more interesting story, though underneath it never wholly lost touch with the more ancient theme of the queen's abduction and recovery.

The patterns which emerge from all of this are very different from the later, idealized medieval stories of 'King' Arthur and his Knights of the Round Table. They are different, also, from the glimpses of the actual historical Arthur, the tough battle-leader with his mobile cavalry force, pitted in deadly combat against the Saxons. Here, as in other texts which deal with the heroic Arthur, his enemies are monsters like Cat Palwc or the hag Pen-Palach, or the mysterious 'dog-men' mentioned in 'Par-Gur?'. The giant Arthur of 'Rhonabwy's Dream' is a distant echo of the historical hero, grown greater in the memory of his people, while the ancient theme of the king and land, represented by the story of Guinevere and Melwas, still shines through.

The Vision of the Mother of God

THE FOLLOWING STORY is based on two previously unconnected episodes, one from the thirteenth-century text Perlesvaus, *the other from the chronicle of* Nennius. *In the former Arthur has a vision of the Virgin, in the latter he is said to have carried a shield with her icon upon it at the great battle of Badon. It seems not unreasonable to connect the two in this way. As in all the stories which are retold here, the themes are traditional to the Matter of Britain. This first story is narrated here by one of the wandering story-tellers who kept the myths of Arthur and the Grail alive throughout the Middle Ages.*

◆ ◆ ◆

YOU WILL HAVE HEARD how at Badon Arthur carried a shield on which was painted an image of the Mother of God. And you will doubtless have been told that this caused the tide of battle to turn in our favour, and that Arthur himself accounted for several hundred of the Saeson that day.

I will not say that this story is a lie, simply that it has grown and changed in the telling. Such is the way with stories, especially after a battle such as Badon, where we finally routed the invaders and pushed them back to the very shores of the island. So it is, also, with men like Arthur, who tend to have stories grow on them like cloaks – until it is sometimes difficult to see the man inside at all.

Like all story-tellers I like to think I know the truth. In this instance I want to tell you how this story about the shield came about, and of the effect it had upon what occurred on that glorious day at Badon.

The story begins when Arthur had not been King for very long. Oh, he had consolidated his power to be sure, had gathered sufficient people to his side to make the unquestioned force in the land. But he had yet to wear the crown officially and have the Bishops mumble their words of blessing over

him. Indeed, he seemed unwilling to do so, declaring that he had yet to prove himself in battle or adventure.

It was for this reason that Arthur decided to visit the chapel in the White Forest. Certainly it had an unchancy reputation, and more than one story I could tell of it that would stir the hair on your heads. But we are speaking of Arthur here, and of Arthur we shall hear.

Having decided to go he told only the Queen and his closest advisers, who of course counselled him not to go at all – or, at least, to take a large company of men with him. But Arthur could be stubborn when he wanted, and the more they insisted the more determined he became to go forth alone. Finally he agreed to take a young squire of the body named Cahus, to see to his needs. He gave instructions to the boy to sleep in the hall that night and to ready his horse as soon as dawn cracked the edge of the sky.

In the night the boy began to dream. He dreamed that he had overslept and that the King had gone without him. And in his dream he saddled his own horse and rode as swiftly as he could into the White Forest. (I know not why it is called by that name, for it is a dark place, where many strange things lurk. Indeed, I believe it to be a part of the Old Wood which existed from the beginning, if the tales I have heard are to be believed . . .)

But I digress. In his dream Cahus arrived before a half-ruined building which had a strange wan light shining out through its single window. Thinking the King must have gone inside to rest, he dismounted and went in himself. There he saw a strange sight. The building was set out like a chapel, with an altar on which stood two elaborate gold candlesticks. In front of the altar lay the body of a richly dressed man, draped in a pall of silk.

The boy was puzzled by this, but even more by the absence of the King, so he took one of the golden candlesticks almost without thinking and went outside again. He mounted his horse and was just about to ride on in search of Arthur, when he saw a huge ugly man approaching. 'Have you seen the King?' demanded the boy. 'I have not. But I have seen you, and the golden relic which you have stolen from the White Chapel, and for that I shall repay you unless you give it back at once.'

Now, let me remind you that all this was the dream of the youth named Cahus. Who, on being addressed thus roughly, suddenly found his pride and refused flatly to give up the candlestick. Then he tried to ride past the big man, who took out a large and wicked-looking knife and stuck it into him, just below the ribs, on the left side . . .

Back in the hall at Carduil, the boy awoke with a scream. His cries soon
awoke the rest of the household, including the King, and when they arrived
in the hall they found the youth lying in a pool of blood, pinned down by
the weight of the huge knife which was stuck into him, while in one hand
he clutched a beautiful golden candlestick . . .

Well, before he died Cahus told the King everything that had happened.
And Arthur gave him his word not only that he would seek out the White
Chapel in the Forest but also that he would exact a full recompense for the
young squire's death. And when Cahus had breathed his last, Arthur called
for his mount and set forth at once, forbidding anyone to follow him.

He rode all day until, as twilight was approaching, he found himself
close to a ruined house in the heart of the forest. And there he dismounted
and tethered his horse and went in. There he saw everything just as Cahus
had described it: the altar, the one remaining candlestick and the body of
the man draped in a rich silken pall. Arthur knelt down and prayed for a
while for the soul of the departed man, then he went back outside and
looked about him for any sign of the ugly man. But the forest was silent
and darkness had begun to fall, so Arthur went back inside the ruined
house and laid out his bed to sleep there in a corner.

Now, I cannot say whether the King dreamed or not, but this is how I
have heard told what took place next. First of all the King thought he heard
voices raised in anger. There were two of them, though he could nowhere
see who they were that spoke. One of them had a fair, kindly voice, while
the other was rough and harsh. And as Arthur listened he learned that they
were arguing over the soul of the dead knight, and from this he guessed
that one was an angel and the other a demon.

Back and forth the quarrel raged, and then there came a little silence, and
a third voice spoke up. It seemed to the King that it must belong to the
most beautiful woman he had ever seen, and it said: 'Depart, and cease this
wrangling. For the soul of this worthy man belongs to us. My son and I
took him into our service five years since, and he has served us well.'

'But', answered the rough voice, 'before that he was an evil man, a
robber and a murderer in this very forest. It is not right that you take him
from me.'

'I do not take him from you,' replied the beautiful voice. 'He had already
chosen to be in our service. If it were not so, he would have come willingly
to you.'

There was a long silence after that and Arthur deemed that the demon had departed. Then, as he lay there in the ruined house he heard the sound of a man chanting the words of the Holy Mass, and when he heard this he sat up and looked around. And all at once the house seemed filled with light, and he could see an aged hermit standing before the altar singing the words of the *introit*. And as the King looked on in wonder he saw that on one side of the hermit stood a child, of no more than six or seven summers, who seemed to him the fairest child he had ever seen. And on the other side, seated in a beautiful chair, sat a woman whose face was so filled with light and joyousness that the King almost could not look upon it.

And as he watched the lady called the child to her and placed him upon her knees. And she said, in the voice which the King knew well, 'Sire, you are my father and my son, my lord and my guardian, and the guardian of everyone.'

And Arthur was filled with wonder at this, and knelt down on the stone floor and joined in the responses of the Mass. And when it came to the *offertorium* he saw the lady offer the child to the hermit, who in turn raised him in his hands above the altar. And at this there came through the window which was behind the altar a spear of such bright light that the King was momentarily blinded. And when he could see again only the hermit stood there, with bowed head, and of the lady and the child there was no sign.

Shaken, Arthur remained for a long time kneeling, until at last the hermit himself helped him to stand and led him outside into the fresh morning air. There he uttered these mysterious words: 'King Arthur. This vision has been granted to you in token of the great adventure of the Grail, which has yet to happen, but which will change the story of this land for ever. Go now, and in the battle that is to come remember what you have seen.'

Arthur could find nothing in him to say by way of answer to this, but solemnly took his leave of the hermit and turned his horse towards Carduil. He had travelled only a little way when he saw standing in his path a huge and ugly man, whom he at once guessed was the same who had slain the boy Cahus in so strange a manner. Arthur drew his sword, so as to be ready, and urged his mount forward.

The big man did not move. His face was grim, and when the King was close to him he said: 'King Arthur, you have in your possession that which belongs to me, and to my brother whose tomb your servant robbed.'

'As to that,' replied the King sternly, 'I have no wish to keep the candlestick. There was no need to kill my squire for it. That I cannot forgive.'

'No more can I forgive the theft of the candlestick,' replied the big man.

'Then let us settle this matter once for all', said Arthur, 'since we both have grievances of the other.'

So Arthur got down from his horse and the two of them dressed their shields to each other and the big man hefted a huge axe in his hand and Arthur attacked with his sword, and the two fought furiously until at last the King got the better of his opponent and slew him. And when the big man fell to the earth the blood which gushed from him was black, and smoked – or so they say – and his body melted away like mist. From which Arthur knew that he had been fighting a demon.

Well, the King rode back to Carduil, without further adventure, and when he was safely within the walls of the great fortress he called to him a certain artisan and required of him that he paint an image of the Mother of God on the inside of his shield.

That was the shield he bore at Badon, and as all here know, he fought as bravely as any man ever did on that day, and led us all to victory over the Saeson. And it is said that whenever his arm grew tired or his spirits sank, the King looked upon the face of the image of the Mother of God within his shield and fought on ever renewed.

As to the mysterious words of the hermit concerning the Grail, that must wait for another night to be told, for there are as many stories of Arthur as there are days in the week and months in the year and years in ages of ages, and even I do not know them all.

·2·
The Hero and the Cauldron: The Beginnings of the Grail in Celtic Tradition

HE BEGINNINGS of the Grail legends are less easy to perceive than those of Arthur. Many versions, both occult and literary, exist. Proposals as varied and curious as their origin in the lost continent of Atlantis to their being a memory of the *krater* or mixing bowl of the gods in Greek myth, have been set forward. Others have declared the Grail to be a bloodline descending from Christ and the Magdalene, the hidden treasure of the Knight's Templar and the secret teaching of the Cathars, a heretical Christian sect of the twelfth century.

All of these things may well be true, for the Grail is many things to many people. What is assuredly so is its importance within the framework of the human story. This is reflected in a number of ways. The sheer proliferation of imagery and the persistent reappearance of the Grail myths from Celtic times to the present mean it is impossible to escape the realization that this is both a deeply embedded and a hugely important strand in the great inner mythology of the West.

THE RAID ON ANNWN

DESPITE CLAIMS for a more primitive point of origin for the Grail, the earliest acceptable written references are from the Celtic tradition. We shall concentrate on these stories as the direct precursors of their full flowering in the Middle Ages.

Before the Grail assumes the form in which we are most used to perceive it – that of a cup or chalice – we find it in the shape of a cauldron. Celtic myth is full of references to such vessels, which are imbued with a

Prospect of Camalet Castle. 15 Aug. 1723.   *Stukeley Del.*

An eighteenth-century engraving for William Stukeley's celebrated 'Itinerary' of Britain: it depicts the Iron Age hill-fort of Cadbury Castle in Somerset, long believed to be the original site of Camelot, Arthur's fabulous city; an archaeological· excavation carried out in the 1960s failed to provide conclusive evidence to support this

variety of magical or miraculous qualities. There is, for example, the Cauldron of Inspiration or *Awen*, guarded by the Welsh corn and fertility goddess Ceridwen. In the 'Story of Taliesin', found in manuscripts dating from the fourteenth century, we hear how it functioned and what happened when someone drank from it.

The story goes that Ceridwen had two children, a son and a daughter. The daughter was astonishingly beautiful and wise; her brother, Avagddu or 'Utter Darkness', was so hideous and stupid that Ceridwen knew he would never achieve anything in the world. And so she set about brewing a drink of knowledge and wisdom which would provide Avagddu with such qualities that no one would notice his looks. To do this she had to brew herbs in her great iron cauldron for a year and a day, and to see that it never ceased from boiling she employed a boy from the nearest village to watch over it.

The year passed quickly and on the last day of all Ceridwen went forth at night to pick the last ingredients for her brew. While she was absent, the boy, whose name was Gwion, sat by the fire and stirred the brew. As he did so three drops of the scalding liquid splashed on to his hand. To lessen the pain of the wound he put his hand to his mouth – and thus imbibed the essence of the drink, which was all concentrated into the three drops.

At once Gwion knew all that there was to know, and among other things he knew that Ceridwen was aware of what had happened through her magic and that she was coming after him in anger. In a justly famous passage the pursuit is described in fantastic detail:

> He saw her, and changed himself into a hare and fled. But she changed herself into a greyhound and turned him. And he ran towards a river, and became a fish. And she in the form of an otter-bitch chased him under the water, until he was fain to turn himself into a bird of the air. She, as a hawk, followed him and gave him no rest in the sky. And just

as she was about to stoop upon him, and he was in fear of death, he espied a heap of winnowed wheat on the floor of a barn, and he dropped among the wheat, and turned himself into one of the grains. Then she transformed herself into a high-crested black hen, and went to the wheat and scratched it with her feet, and found him out and swallowed him. And, as the story says, she bore him nine months, and when she was delivered of him, she could not find it in her heart to kill him for reason of his beauty. So she wrapped him in a leathern bag, and cast him into the sea . . . on the twenty-ninth day of April.

(Guest)

The Prophet Merlin Dictating his Prophecies to his Scribe, from a fifteenth-century wood-cut

The bag floated in the sea for nine nights and nine days until it came to rest on the pole of a salmon weir belonging to a prince of Dyfed named Gwyddno. And it happened that on that day the prince's son Elphin came to collect the rich catch of salmon which was supposed to be there. But all he found was a leather bag hanging from the weir, and when he opened it he saw within the face of a beautiful child. Light seemed to come from the brow of the child, and Elphin exclaimed: 'Behold, a radiant brow!' From within the bag came the child's voice, declaring 'Taliesin [*tal-iessin*. "radiant brow"] shall I be called!'

And so Gwion became Taliesin, and was renowned for his wisdom and his skill as a bard, leaving many poems which are still extant. In this story, as well as in the works attributed to him, we can see the remains of a far more ancient, shamanistic tradition which was once prevalent in these islands (see J. Matthews, 1990h).

The source of this wisdom is seen as originating in the Cauldron of Ceridwen, which contained the essence of all knowledge. It is the first of several such vessels which predate the Grail but exemplify many of its later attributes. Another is the Hamper or Basket of Gwyddno (the same who possessed the salmon weir), which had the quality that although only enough food for one was put into it, enough for 100 could be taken out. In other words, it is a container of plenty, an inexhaustible fund of good things – another of the Grail's later attributes.

But perhaps the most famous of these early Celtic vessels of wonder is the Cauldron of Annwn. References to this abound within early Celtic literature and tradition. From the point of view of our present investigation, the most important is in a poem attributed to Taliesin (who better to tell of one of the great cauldrons?), dated to the ninth century. In fact, it contains elements from an earlier oral tradition and certainly dates back much further, perhaps to Arthur's time or even before. However, in the form in which it has come down to us, Arthur is very clearly identified as the foremost hero, who in this instance is in search of the wondrous cauldron for himself. This is in keeping with the picture of the heroic Arthur whom we first encountered in the previous chapter. That he is discovered entering the realm of the Otherworld in quest of a wonder-working vessel is of considerable significance to the history of the Grail. Indeed, it is the earliest text referring to such a search in which Arthur and his heroes are involved. Though it is obscurely written in medieval Welsh, making the details of the story at times hard to follow, it is none the less worth quoting in full:

Preiddeu Annwn
(Spoils of the In-World)

In Caer Siddi Gwair's prison was readied,
As Pwyll and Pryderi foretold,
None before went there save he,
Where the heavy chains bound him.
Before the spoiling of Annwn he sang for ever
This eternal invocation of poets:
Save only seven, none returned from Caer Siddi.

Since my song resounded in the turning Caer,
I am pre-eminent. My first song
Was of the Cauldron itself.
Nine maidens kindled it with their breath –
Of what nature was it?
Pearls were about its rim,
it would not boil a coward's portion.
Lleminawg thrust his flashing sword
Deep within it;
And before dark gates, a light was lifted.
When we went with Arthur – a mighty labour –
Save only seven, none returned from Caer Fedwydd.

I am pre-eminent
Since my song resounded
In the four-square city [Caer Pedruven],
In the island of the Strong Door.
The light was dim and mixed with darkness,
Though bright wine was set before us.
Three shiploads of *Prydwen* went with Arthur –
Save only seven, none returned from Caer Rigor.

Worth more am I than the clerks
Who have not seen Arthur's might
Beyond Caer Siddi.
Six thousand stood on its walls –
It was hard to speak with their leader.
Three shiploads of *Prydwen* went with Arthur –
Save seven only, none returned from Caer Goludd.

I merit more than empty bards
Who know not the day, the hour or the moment
When the chick was born;
Who have not journeyed
To the courts of heaven;
Who know nothing of the meaning
Of the starry-collared ox
With seven score links in his collar.
When we went with Arthur – that sorrowful journey –
Save seven only, none returned from Manawyddan's Caer.

I know more for ever than the weak willed clerks
Who know not the day of the King's birth,
Nor the nature of the beast they guard for him.
When we went with Arthur – lamentable day –
Save only seven, none returned from Caer Achren.

We are not told the names of the seven men who survived this mysterious voyage. Arthur is one clearly; Taliesin himself – since he is telling the story – is another. The identities of the rest we can only guess at, though it is reasonable to suppose that Lleminawg (possibly the original Lancelot) may be another, and possibly Bedwyr and Cai, Arthur's most stalwart supporters, are two more. Indeed, the whole story is really only hinted at. We can see that the cauldron is probably tended by nine women – possibly priestesses – whose breath warms the vessel's rim. We know there are warriors to the

Queen Guinevere by Walter Crane

Looking towards
Glastonbury from the 'Thorn
Gate' on Cadbury Camp
(*John Rogers*)

tune of 6,000 led by a mysterious individual with whom it was hard to
converse. We are told nothing about the cauldron itself, or even whether
the raid is successful. All we do know is that there are seven islands or
cities to which the voyagers go in search of their prize, each of which contains a further test.

Indeed, this intricate and mysterious work can be interpreted in many
ways: as a map of the states of the shaman, journeying into the inner
realms in quest of knowledge; as different states of being on the soul's
journey through life. The names of the seven islands through which the
heroes pass on their way to reive the cauldron, when translated, also
suggest an interesting progression:

1	Caer Achren –	The City of the Trees
2	Caer Manawyddan –	The City of the Sea (-God)
3	Caer Goludd –	The City of Riches
4	Caer Rigor –	The City of Frustration
5	Caer Fedwydd –	The City of Celebration
6	Caer Pedruven –	The Four-Sided City
7	Caer Siddi –	The City of Glass

Each of these names is capable of more than one interpretation. Caer Siddi is a name frequently given to the Otherworld, as is Caer Manawyddan. Viewed as a series of stages in the path of the seeker or initiate, the poem as a whole makes a satisfying pattern.

1   The City of the Trees
This is Middle Earth, represented by the great forest through which the seeker wanders until she or he finds a way of leaving behind the entangling webs of the earthly realm and of ascending to:

2   The City of the Sea
This is the realm of the god Manawyddan, the watery state of being which often precludes movement from one elemental state to another – in this case from earth to water. It, in turn, leads to:

3   The City of Riches
Here the seeker tastes the delights of awakening in the realm of the spirit which makes it possible to enter every part of creation at once. Not everything will be understood, but sufficient will be realized to enable movement to the next stage:

4   The City of Frustration
Here the seeker learns that despite the richness of new awareness she or he has to master her/himself and to govern completely the power which will enable her/him to realize the full potential of the next city:

5   The City of Celebration
Here at last the seeker is able to partake completely of the richness perceived in the third city. Here begins the celebration of the mastery over understanding. Identity with the natural world is almost complete, and the way is opened to the penultimate stage:

6   The Four-Sided City
Here an ultimate degree of understanding is revealed; the four elements, the four directions and the four winds are bound together and through their interaction the final gift of empowerment takes place. The seeker is able to enter the last of the seven cities:

7   The City of Glass
In Caer Siddi the seeker enters the innermost realm of Annwn, the In-World, the place from where it is possible to look out and study all the manifest forms of creation, from whence the seeker becomes aware of all possibilities.

This is a pattern which, as we shall see, is reflected in the later Grail romances, and implies a strong heritage of common elements in both. The

Queen Guinevere Goes A-Maying by Louis Rhead. Guinevere, accompanied by her knights, went to gather May blossoms; she was abducted by Sir Meleagraunce and later rescued by Sir Lancelot

cauldron itself is here given no specific set of attributes beyond the fact that it will not boil food for a coward – an important factor among a race so utterly given over to personal bravery. These same qualities are inherited in enhanced form in the later medieval legends, where the Grail can be won only by the worthiest knight, and where it frequently provides the food most desired by those who see it.

For a further indication of the possible qualities it possesses, we must turn to another text which, though seemingly unconnected, actually supplies several missing states in the story, clarifying it considerably in the process.

THE CAULDRON OF REBIRTH

THIS TEXT, 'The Story of Branwen', is another from *The Mabinogion* collection. The main part of the story does not concern us here: one or two incidents, however, are important. The first concerns the gift of a certain cauldron from Bentigeid Vran (Bran the Blessed), King of Britain, to Matholwch, King of Ireland, in settlement of a quarrel. The nature of this cauldron is that 'If one of thy men be slain to-day, and be cast therein, to-morrow he will be as well as ever he was at the best, except that he will not regain his speech' (Guest).

But there is more to the nature of this gift than is at first evident. First we learn that the wondrous vessel originated in Ireland itself. Matholwch tells the following story:

> One day I was hunting in Ireland, and I came to the mound at the head of the lake which is called the Yellow Lake of the Cauldron. And I beheld a huge yellow-haired man coming from the lake with a cauldron upon his back. And he was a man of vast size, and of horrid aspect, and a woman followed after him. And if the man was tall, twice as large as he was the woman, and they came towards me and greeted me.
>
> (Guest)

The huge man explains that the woman is soon to give birth, and that when she does so it will be to a fully armed warrior. Matholwch declares that no pregnant woman shall go without food or shelter at such a time, and takes them home with him. They soon make themselves so unpopular with their monstrous behaviour that Matholwch's people demand that he get rid of them. He does so by the bizarre method of building a house of white bronze in which he secures his unwelcome guests and then sets fire beneath it, until the walls are glowing with heat. At this point the giant man and his wife break out and flee, taking the cauldron with them and setting sail for Britain. There Bran gave them shelter and, on discovering that the woman gave birth every six weeks to a fully armed warrior, used them to garrison his strong fortresses.

This bizarre tale has several points of interest. The cauldron, we are told, gives back life to dead warriors. The giant woman gives birth to fully armed men. Although the names of the giant couple are given as Llassar Llaes Gyfnewydd and Cymeidi Cymeinfoll, it is evident that the owners of the cauldron are reflections of Ceridwen and her mate, Tegid Foel, both of whom are seen as coming from a lake (Llyn Tegid) and who possess a remarkable vessel. If we put all of this together, a pattern begins to emerge. The cauldron is clearly a life-giving vessel which enables warriors to return from the Otherworld alive but unable to speak of their experience – a further suggestion of some kind of initiation of which it was, of course, forbidden to speak. The heating of the bronze house to destroy the giant and his wife is a direct inversion of the cauldron itself, bringing death rather than giving life.

Nor does the story end there. Later on in the same text, we are told that when relations worsen between Bran and Matholwch, the former leads an army to retrieve the cauldron. In the ensuing mêlée Evnissien, Bran's troublesome brother, destroys both the cauldron and himself by climbing into it – a living man – and stretching out until he breaks both his heart and the vessel. And, the story continues,

The Cauldron-Born

In consequence of that the men of the Island of the Mighty (Britain) obtained such success as they had; but they were not victorious, for *only seven men of them all escaped,* and Bendegeid Vran himself was wounded in the foot with a poisoned dart. Now the seven men that escaped were Pryderi, Manawyddan, Gleneu Eli Taran, Taliesin, Ynawc, Gruyden the son of Muryel, and Heilyn the son of Gwenn Hen.

(Guest; my italics)

Is it too much to suppose that here we have a reference to the story also found in the *Preiddeu Annwn*? Once again the quest is for a cauldron of great worth and magical properties. The leader is a king, and only seven men return, among whom is Taliesin. The parallels are clear enough, and the nature of the cauldron, which is to restore the dead to life, connects not only with other wonder-working vessels of Celtic tradition but also, as we shall see, with the Grail itself. In addition, the wounding of Bran in the foot, and the events which follow it, will be seen in Chapter 3 to be part of a highly significant theme.

THE DAMSELS OF THE WELLS

CELTIC TRADITION continued to be a powerful influence on the developing Grail mythos throughout the Middle Ages, and many of the primary themes within the cycles of stories can be traced back to these early beginnings. For this reason two texts which actually date from much later will be considered here for the sake of clarity. Despite the fact that they were not written down until the twelfth century, both betray a far earlier origin in oral tradition or lost originals and represent earlier strands of the Grail tradition.

The first is written in Old French and was published in Paris in 1530 under the title '*Elucidation de l'hystoire du Graal*', though it has since been dated to somewhere between 1220 and 1225 (Evans). Essentially it presents itself as a prequel to the more famous twelfth-century poem by Chrétien de Troyes, *Perceval, ou Le Conte du Graal* (*Perceval, or The Story of the Grail*), which is considered one of the pre-eminent sources for all Grail traditions. This will be considered fully in the next chapter. In fact, the '*Elucidation*', as we shall call it, neither elucidates nor, indeed, connects to Chrétien's poem at all. It is a curious and sometimes confusing work which has none the less succeeded in preserving a far earlier story of the Grail than its successors do.

The work opens with the following strange injunction:

Sir Gawain in *The Mule without a Bridle* by Thomas Bewick, from an eighteenth-century book, Way's *Fabliaux* (1796). In this medieval fable, Gawain encounters a fearsome dragon

Here worshipfully begins a romance of the most delightful story of the Graal, the secret of which no man may tell in verse or prose, for so might the story turn out before it is fully told, that all men might be grieved by it. Because of which wise men leave it aside and simply pass on to other things, for if Master Blihis tells it truthfully, this secret no man should know.

Having told us that the story should not be told, the author – who is possibly the mysterious 'Master Blihis' himself – begins to tell how 'the rich country of Logres, of which there was much talk in ancient times, came to be destroyed'.

The kingdom turned to loss, the land was dead and desert so that it was scarcely worth two hazel-nuts. For they had lost the voices of the wells and the damsels that lived therein. For no less a thing was the service they gave than this – that if anyone wandered that way, whether at evening or morning, rather than that he should go far out of his way for food and drink, he should find his way to the wells, and then no better could he ask but that he received it at once. For straightway a damsel issued forth from the well, none fairer need he seek, bearing in her hand a cup of gold . . . and right fair welcome he received at the well.

This custom apparently continued for some time, until

King Amangons, who was evil and craven-hearted, was the first to break the custom, for thereafter many took their lead from this king, whose duty it was to protect the damsels and to maintain and guard them

within his peace. But he forced one of the damsels, and carried off from her the cup of gold she had and ever after caused himself to be served from it daily. . . . Thereafter the damsel never served anyone else who came there in search of food. And all the other damsels only served in such a way that they were invisible to all.

Following King Amangons' evil act, many other damsels of the wells were raped by his knights, who carried off their golden cups until there were none left to serve passing travellers. The results of this were plain to see:

In such a way was the Kingdom laid waste that from thenceforward was no tree leafy. The meadows and flowers were dried up and the waters were shrunken, and no man might then find the Court of the Rich Fisherman, which was wont to make within the land a glittering glory of gold and silver, ermine and minaver, rich palls of sendal, meats and stuffs, falcons gentle and merlins and tercels and sparrow-hawks and falcons peregrine.

As long as this court is present, the whole of the land flourishes, but when it is lost the kingdom founders. And so matters continue until Arthur's time, when the brave, honest and hardy knights hear of the damsels and at once determine to discover both the wells and the Court of the Rich Fisherman for themselves. They set forth into the forest and there discover a marvellous thing: the descendants of the damsels who were raped by Amangons and his men are still living there. One of them, a knight named Blihos Blihiris (a name curiously similar to that of the supposed author of the work) is a great story-teller, and he tells the whole story from beginning to end. Arthur's knights are angered and swear to recover the wells and the court, from whence shall come the joy with which the land shall again be made bright.

> Right stoutly they sought the Court of the Rich Fisherman, who knew much of necromancy, and could change his appearance a hundred times, in such wise that those who knew him in one guise would not recognize him in another.
>
> Gawain found the court in Arthur's time, as shall be told in full, and of the joy that came about as a result, but before him a young knight found it . . . named Perceval of Wales. He asked whom the Graal served, but demanded not of the Lance, when he saw it . . . nor of the Sword, of which one half was missing and the other lay on a bier with the body of one who was dead . . .

View from the summit of Dinas Emrys, showing part of the ruins which may be all that remain of Vortigern's ill-fated castle (*Tim Cann*)

The story then goes on to discuss, in rather a cryptic manner, the other mysteries of the Grail, which we shall return to in the next chapter. For the moment, let us look back over this curious story as it is told to this point.

What are we to make of these damsels of the wells, who offer hospitality to passing travellers, giving them food and drink from their golden cups? If we turn to Celtic tradition we see at once that these are Otherworldly women, people of the *Sidhe*, who hold keys to the realms of enchantment. References abound to such faery women, who appear and lead mortals into the inner realms, and who sometimes offer not only what is referred to as 'the hospitality of the thighs' but also a deeper enchantment. In the Irish story of *Baille in Scaile*, for example, the hero Conn is actually abducted into the Otherworld in order that he may receive a vision of his future kingly destiny.

> They went into a house of gold and saw a girl seated in a chair of crystal, wearing a golden crown. In front of her was a silver vat with corners of gold. A vessel of gold stood beside her and before her was a golden cup. . . . The girl was the Sovranty of Ireland and she gave food to Conn . . .

> (Dillon)

When the girl goes to serve ale to the company, she asks to whom the cup of red ale – Dergflaith, the Red Drink of Lordship – should be given, and is told to offer it to Conn as a sign that he will be king.

Here the vessel confers the essence of sovereignty, the gift of the land over which Conn will one day rule. The Grail offers a more spiritual essence, but the underlying truth is the same, and the women who offer a drink from their cups to the passing stranger are only a small remove from the girl who is the sovereignty of Ireland.

In the context of the '*Elucidation*', of course, they have been reduced to mysterious and inexplicable servants, their original roles lost in the reshaping of the story. Yet there are still glimpses of their origins: for example, after Amangons has raped one of their number the rest continue to serve, but invisibly, and they are said to 'come forth from the wells', making it clear that they are not simply dwelling in some hut beside the source of water.

More important than this is their connection to the land. Once the 'custom' has been broken by Amangons, whose men soon follow suit, the land becomes a desert, dry and unfruitful, where there are no leaves on the trees and the meadows dry up. This is a vital clue to the origin of the Grail in Celtic tradition, and incidentally it ushers in one of the constant themes of the Grail stories hereafter – the Waste Land, and its causes.

Essentially, in Celtic tradition the king and the land are one, so closely related that when one falls sick the other is affected. Thus only a king perfect in body can rule the land; if he is maimed or wounded, as in the case of Lugh Lamfada, who lost a hand in battle and was given a new one of silver, another has to take over the kingdom.

This theme runs through all of the Arthurian Grail texts, and is of

The arms of Arthur and his most famous knights, as depicted in a seventeenth-century armorial from France

primary importance to an understanding of the stories. Nowhere is it more clearly demonstrated than here, I believe, in this curious text with its confused twists and turns.

Equally mysterious – though enlightening in this context – are the Rich Fisherman and his court, which dispenses goodness and plenty throughout the land. The author makes it clear that the quest for this place is of great importance, and that its finding will bring a kind of restoration to the wasted land of Logres. As for the Rich Fisherman himself, we shall meet him often throughout our exploration of the Grail stories, though never quite as in the depiction here. In the more familiar medieval stories we shall be examining in the succeeding chapters, the Fisherman, or, as he is more often called, the Fisher King, is an ancient, holy man who suffers from an unhealing wound which only the destined Grail winner can heal. Here we see him as a shape-shifter and magician figure, more akin to the Celtic god of the sea, Manannan mac Lir, who also has the ability to change his shape.

Equally interesting, in the context of the Celtic Grail stream, is the statement that Gawain was the one who discovered the court. Gawain is the pre-eminent Celtic hero of Arthur's court, originally far outranking Lancelot, Kay or Bedivere in terms of popularity. I have argued at length elsewhere (J. Matthews, 1990d) that he is the oldest of the Grail winners, and this reference seems to bear me out. Though we are told that it is the young Perceval who asks the all-important question concerning the Grail, the sword and the spear, this does not detract from Gawain's personal success.

Gawain is Arthur's cousin and, like Culhwch in the story discussed in Chapter 1, he is purely Celtic in his origins and behaviour. His presence alone would lead one to suppose a Celtic connection in this text. The underlying myth of the wells and the damsels who served at them is an even stronger indication of this. Sacred wells abound in Celtic tradition and are nearly always a gateway to the Otherworld. We often hear, for example, of the Well of Segais, which rises in this world but whose waters contain the essence of Otherworldly power and wisdom. In the '*Elucidation*' we are hearing the last dying echo of a very ancient theme: the wells are guarded by a chosen band of priestesses whose task it is to keep open the ways between the worlds and act as 'voices' for the mysteries of the Otherworld. As such they are sacred, and when one of them is abused – soon to be followed by many others – not only is the land wounded but the voices fall silent; there is no longer communication between the two worlds. It could be said that our world has never recovered from this severing of ancient ties, and as a result we still suffer from the loss of a deeper and more ancient harmony with the land and with the living earth beneath us. The quest of Arthur's knights is therefore very much our own quest for wholeness – as indeed is the quest for the Grail in all of the stories. The offer of hope – the joy of the court – is surely one of the reasons for the continued fascination with the Grail. Here, in this curious little work and despite many borrowings from later sources, something like a beginning is preserved.

The story of the quest itself, here only hinted at, is told and retold in many ways. For the version nearest in its essence to the Celtic way, we must turn now to a very different text.

THE REVENGE OF PEREDUR

THE STORY OF *Peredur mab Efrawg* is found in the collection which goes by the title of *The Mabinogion*. It offers something of a problem in that no one can decide whether it came before or after Chrétien de Troyes's *Perceval, ou Le Conte du Graal* – generally considered to be the first Grail text proper. However, the story of Peredur, while substantially the same as that of Perceval, differs in so many ways from the French poem that it deserves to be considered as a separate composition, and this we shall do. Laying aside the question of its date for the moment, there can be little doubt that, like the '*Elucidation*', it preserves a much earlier version of the story.

The Earl of Efrawg had seven sons, all of whom were killed, along with their father, in battle. All, this is, save one, Peredur, the youngest. His mother is determined that he should know nothing of arms or warfare, and brings him up in seclusion in the forest. However, as he grows to young manhood he displays a natural skill with a spear and bow, and this makes him a great hunter. One day as he wanders in the forest he espies

A cave near Wetton Mill, Staffordshire, said by local tradition to be the site of Gawain's encounter with the fearsome Green Knight (*Tim Cann*)

three warriors who seem so wonderful that he runs back at once to ask his mother what they are. She tells him they are angels and warns him against following them. But he is determined to go, and since nothing she can say will dissuade him, his mother gives him some sage advice. She tells him that he should say a prayer whenever he sees a church, take food and drink whenever he needs them, even if they are not offered, and go to the aid of any woman who cries out in distress; if he sees a jewel he should take it and offer it to another, and he should always pay court to beautiful women. Peredur fashions makeshift weapons and, riding an old spavined horse, sets out to follow the warriors he had met in the forest. On the way he sees a tent in which is an unattended maiden. He helps himself to food and drink, steals a ring from the maiden and kisses her before riding on. When her guardian, the Proud Knight of the Clearing, returns, he accuses her of faithlessness and swears she will never after remain in the same place more than two nights.

Peredur, meanwhile, arrives at Arthur's court, where he witnesses a knight throw wine into Gwenhwyfar's lap. Cai mocks him but two dwarfs, who had hitherto never spoken, greet him as the best of knights. Cai strikes the dwarfs and orders Peredur to follow the knight who had insulted the Queen. He does so and, having dispatched the man with ease, tries to drag him out of his armour. Fortunately Owein, one of Arthur's best knights, arrives and advises him. Peredur refuses to return to court until he has proved himself further. He goes on his way and defeats sixteen knights, sending them all back to Arthur. Arriving at a lake, he sees a richly dressed old man and two youths fishing from a boat. The old man reveals that he is Peredur's maternal uncle, and at his invitation the young man stays at his court and is instructed in the proper use of arms. When the time comes for him to depart he receives more advice. This time he is told not to ask unnecessary questions.

Riding on his way Peredur arrives at another court, ruled over by an old man who also reveals himself as a maternal uncle. There Peredur is invited to break an iron column with a sword. Each time he strikes, both sword and column break; twice they reunite, but the third time they remain broken. The old man says this means that his nephew has reached only two-thirds of his strength.

As they sit at supper that night a spear is carried into the hall and from its point drops of blood fall. This is followed by a platter on which is a man's head floating in blood. Mindful of his other uncle's advice, Peredur fails to ask the meaning of either. Next morning he rides off and hears a maiden cry out. She is mourning a dead knight, her husband. Addressing Peredur, she accuses him of causing his mother's death, for she has died of sorrow after his departure. The maiden herself is Peredur's foster-sister. At this juncture the man responsible for the death of her husband appears, and Peredur overcomes him, forcing him to promise he will marry the maiden and submit to Arthur. He sends a message with the man to Cai, that he will avenge the affront to the two dwarfs, whom his foster-sister had revealed were once servants to Peredur's father.

Arthur is so impressed by Peredur's deeds that he decides to go in search of him and persuade him to return to court and heal the breach with Cai. Meanwhile, Peredur reaches a castle, where he is greeted by a girl dressed in rags. Her goods have been confiscated by a young Earl who wishes to marry her. That night her brothers send her to Peredur's bedroom, but he rebuffs her. Next day he defeats the Earl and makes him restore the girl's lands. He then meets and overcomes the Proud Knight of the Clearing and bids him forgive his lady, who is innocent.

Peredur continues on until he comes to a mountain castle where a tall woman rules. She warns him that she is being terrorized by a group of nine hags. Peredur stays anyway and next morning encounters one of the hags, whom he strikes. She recognizes him and says that it has been prophesied that she will teach him greater skill with arms. He stays with her for three weeks, then sets out again.

On his way he sees a sight which transfixes him: a wild duck lies dead in the snow with a raven feeding off it. The redness of the blood, the whiteness of the snow and the blackness of the raven's plumage reminds him him of a woman he loves. Rapt in his vision, he does not see Arthur and his men approaching, Cai rides forward and tries to arouse him. Absentmindedly Peredur knocks him down. With gentler words Gwalchmai

The Bertinus Chalice (1222), now in the Metropolitan Museum of Art, New York: one of several cups believed to be the actual 'Holy Grail'

Arthur and his companions
in the ship *Prydwen*, after an
illustration in *Estoire de Merlin*
(Bologna, early fourteenth
century)

(Gawain) breaks the reverie and Peredur realizes that he has avenged the
insult to the two dwarfs. He agrees to return to court.

While there he falls in love with Angharad Golden-Hair, who rejects
him. He refuses to speak to anyone until she acknowledges him and then
sets out on his way again. He meets and overcomes a party of giants, slays
a serpent and acquires the ring it was guarding. Growing tired of his own
company, he then sets out to return to court again. On the way he meets
Cai, who professes not to recognize him and strikes him three times, finally
wounding him in the thigh. After a further adventure with a ferocious
knight, he returns to Caerleon, where Angharad finally recognizes his suit.

While out hunting with Arthur, Peredur comes to a hall in the wilder-
ness where lives the Black Oppressor and his daughters. The eldest begs
Peredur to leave and causes her father to refrain from attacking him. The
man tells how he lost an eye while fighting the Black Serpent of the
Dolorous Mound. This creature guards a stone which, when held in one
hand, gives as much gold as required in the other. Perceval then fights the
Black Oppressor and overcomes him, obtaining directions to the Dolorous
Mound.

Setting out, he visits the King of Suffering, so called because a water
monster daily consumes one of his sons, who is then revived in a bath of
water. Peredur undertakes to defeat the monster. He meets a beautiful
woman sitting on a mound, who offers him a ring of invisibility in return
for his undying love.

Next he comes to a valley divided by a river. One one side of the river
are black sheep, on the other white. Whenever one crosses the river it
changes colour. On the bank is a tree, one half in flames, the other in green
leaf. Peredur continues until he reaches the cave of the monster and slays
it. The sons of the King of Suffering beg him to marry one of their sisters,

but he refuses. Continuing on, he finally reaches the Dolorous Mound and slays the serpent, giving the magical stone to a companion.

Peredur next arrives at a valley full of mills, where he encounters the beautiful woman who had given him the ring of invisibility which had enabled him to defeat the serpent and the water monster. While they are talking three men in succession enter with three cups: one plain, the other shaped like a monster's claw, the third made of gold. Peredur defeats all three and keeps their cups. He then remains with the woman for fourteen years.

One day as Arthur is at Caerleon with Peredur a hideous woman rides into court and berates Peredur for not asking about the spear and head in the dish at his uncle's court. This had been the cause of great suffering. Determined to find out the truth, Peredur rides out in search of the hideous damsel. He has many more adventures before finally arriving at a castle where an old man is sitting in a hall. A youth enters and explains that he was the hideous woman and that he is really Peredur's cousin. He says that the spear had been used to lame the Fisherman and that the head in the dish was Peredur's own first cousin, whose death he is destined to avenge on the nine black hags of Gloucester, one of whom Peredur had met earlier when she trained him in arms. With the help of Arthur and his men, especially Gwalchmai, Peredur fights and kills the hags, thus avenging his uncle and cousin and setting right the wrongs which had been done by them.

A replica of the lead cross reputedly discovered at Glastonbury bearing the inscription 'Here lies buried the body of King Arthur in the Island of Avalon'

This long and complex work contains so many threads of the tapestry which makes up the Grail story that I have chosen to give a much fuller summary than would normally be the case. Despite the fact that it more or less follows the outline of Chrétien's text, and despite a thin veneer of Christianity and medieval chivalry, it bears the stamp of Celtic tradition throughout. The 'quest' element here is not for a spiritual goal, or even for inspiration or the restoration of life; it is, aside from an initial goal of adventure and fame, pure and simple revenge. Peredur avenges the death of one uncle and the wounding of another on the nine hags of Gloucester. He is helped throughout by a series of Otherworldly people – the old Fisherman, whom of course we have already encountered in the 'Elucidation', and the mysterious woman who is able to give him the gift of invisibility and with whom he spends fourteen years (possibly in the Otherworld itself and therefore outside time – assuredly no time seems to pass between this adventure and the next). And he passes through a landscape which is certainly not of this earth – where black and white sheep change colour by crossing a stream, and where a tree is seen that is one half in green leaf and the other in flames.

This is all a far cry from the wonders of the later Grail texts, and despite being written down in the fourteenth century, it bears all the hallmarks of being based on one or more oral tales of the kind that went into the melting pot which produced *The Mabinogion* itself and retained the memory of even more ancient tales once widely known in the Celtic realms.

Peredur himself is a far cry from the courtly heroes of the medieval Arthur cycles. He is rough, rude, foolish and often savage. He loves fighting and women, and has a powerful contact with the natural world. He is given to fits of abstraction as profound – and as dangerous to those who interrupt him – as any experienced by Celtic heroes such as Cuchulainn or Fionn.

Just how much of the story itself draws upon the medieval Grail and Arthur romances, and how much contains the raw materials from which these were themselves created, the reader must judge. In the next chapter we shall look at some of the first of these great tales which grew – in time and with the play of historical forces – into the shining tales of Arthur and the Round Table.

The Voyage to Annwn

THIS STORY is based squarely on the poem quoted on pages 43–4. It has been fleshed out from hints and guesses contained in other texts, and from a general understanding of Celtic myth and the quest for the Grail. As in the previous tale, it is told by a wandering bard or story-teller, perhaps visiting the castle of a nobleman hungry for more stories of Arthur. In this instance he chooses to tell an older version of the ever popular Grail quest.

◆ ◆ ◆

THE STORY OF ARTHUR'S VOYAGE to Annwn used to be told everywhere in the land, but in more recent times another has taken its place and I have not heard it in many years. So shall I tell it tonight, for it is a good tale, well worth the telling, and it holds a truth which is best not forgotten, even in these times.

It begins one time when Arthur was at Carlisle, where the dark forest of Inglewood washes almost up to the walls, only stopping a league or so distant, as though it wanted to overwhelm the great city, but thought better of it. There it was that the great bard Taliesin came, and that night in the great hall, by the light of the flickering torches, he told the tale of the old god Bran, and of his magic cauldron which could bring the dead back to life – though dumb, so that they could not speak of what they had seen beyond the edge of death's curtain. And as he told the tale, few noticed how the King leaned forward in his chair, his eyes gleaming with a light which was perhaps no more than the reflection of the torches, but which seemed to come from within.

And, in the weeks that followed, Arthur became increasingly remote, dealing as ever with matters of state, but seeming to have little or no time for other things. At last, he called round him his closest advisers, and spoke his thoughts aloud.

'It is my wish,' he said, 'to make a journey. It will be a dangerous one and I will ask only those who desire it to accompany me.'

Taliesin, who was numbered among the wise guardians of the land,

asked: 'To what place would you journey, my lord?'

Arthur smiled openly. 'Why, to Annwn,' he said, naming the name that struck terror into the hearts of most men in those days. For this was the Otherworld, ruled over by Arawn himself, the dark lord who hunted the lands above and beneath with his pack of red-eared, white-bodied hounds. None living had ever entered that place and returned to tell of it, save only Pwyll, who, it was said, had once exchanged places with Arawn and served as king in that land for year.*

'Why would you seek to go there?' asked another of the advisers in wonderment. Fear was writ large upon all their faces.

'I seek the cauldron that Bran the Blessed once owned. For it is well known that after his death, when the Feasting of the Noble Head was over, it was carried beneath the land and given into the keeping of Arawn himself. There it still rests, and there I would journey to discover it.'

The royal counsellors were silent for a time. Then Taliesin suddenly laughed. 'And why not?' said he, 'I have long wished to see the lands beneath for myself. I, for one, will go.'

And so it was that when the next new moon rose above the Island of the Mighty, Arthur set sail in his ship *Prydwen*, accompanied by a crew of thirty men – the best, it was said, of the warriors of the island, and including Taliesin himself.

They sailed north, for in those days it was known that the entrance to Annwn lay somewhere beyond the northernmost edge of the land. Two weeks of rough weather and wild water brought them at last to a place where the waters suddenly became still. The wind dropped and *Prydwen*'s sails hung empty. The crew broke out the oars and began to row forward steadily – though there was none there save perhaps Arthur himself, and Taliesin, who did not look over his shoulders as they went, for the air of that place became steadily thicker, until it was palpable and difficult to breathe, and a darkness more tangible than that of night grew deeper around them.

How long they continued in this manner none could say. Time itself had no meaning in that place. But at length Taliesin cried aloud where he sat in the prow, keeping watch for them all. And as they all looked where he looked they saw, far off, like a star in that lightless place, a light.

---

*This story is told in *The Mabinogion*.

Scarcely moving now, so intense was the darkness and so thick the air, the ship sailed on, driven by the slow, deep strokes of her oars. And as she went, gradually the darkness began to lift, until it was possible to see something of their surroundings.

Around them the water lay flat and black as a mirror with nothing but darkness to reflect, all the way to the feet of a great outcrop of rock which rose sheer into the sky for hundreds of feet. The light they had seen came from here, and by its bleak radiance they saw walls and towers, pinnacles and turrets of black, adamantine stone. Leading to that towering edifice was a path of water, flanked by six vast pillars not unlike the first, though smaller.

A light had dawned in the King's eyes, almost as fierce as that which burned far above them. He gave the order to move forward, and though there was not a man who cared to do so, yet they all answered to their lord's will and pushed the ship onward towards the towers of Annwn.

When no more than a league separated them from the frowning cliffs, the water ahead suddenly began to boil, as though it were itself a great cauldron, and as the warriors stared there rose from the sea a huge and terrible head. Serried ranks of teeth gleamed in a mouth large enough to swallow *Prydwen*. Two great luminous eyes glared down upon them, as the head rose higher and higher into the air, carried on a huge and gleaming neck.

Men cried out in fear, and Arthur drew his great sword Excalibur. The monstrous head drove in upon them and when it lifted again a third of *Prydwen*'s crew were gone, swallowed by that dreadful maw. The air was filled with a high keening that echoed from the rocks on every side and was magnified a thousandfold.

Strange shapes danced in the air around the ship. Faces there were, seeming like long-drowned men, their flesh half eaten or rotted away. Several of the crew leapt screaming over the side to vanish for ever into the darkly swirling tide. *Prydwen* leapt and wallowed and took in water until she was in danger of sinking entirely beneath the sea.

Then the creature rose again above them, its vast bulk cleaving the water and its monstrous jaws gaping wide. The warriors cowered in the sculls, holding their weapons above them in a vain hope of fending off the dread creature. Only Taliesin stood calmly in the bow, and he raised his voice in a great chant. The words themselves were strange even to those who knew him, being in a tongue more ancient than that of the court. Their effect

The Guardian of Annwn

upon the monster was immediate. Its eyes and mouth closed and it gave vent to a bellow which rocked the ship and set men to covering their ears. Then it rose high above them, its vast body showing almost entire above the water. Streams of water crashed upon the deck of *Prydwen*, and mighty waves thundered against her sides, but as the monster sank again the sea slowly settled back to its former calm.

Shaken, the men leaned upon their oars, as a great stillness fell once more around them. More than half the crew were gone. Then Arthur, murmuring his thanks to the Bard, raised his head again to the tower rising above them. There he saw something which caused him to fall silent. All there followed his gaze, and saw a mighty figure outlined on the cliffs above. Utterly dark it seemed, from its night-dark clothing to the black iron helm which masked its face. From within, carried easily on the air, came a cold voice.

'Who dares enter the Cauldron of Annwn?'

And Arthur answered. 'It is Arthur who comes, and with me the warriors of the Island of the Mighty.'

There was silence for a moment, then the voice came again: 'Step up, little King, and let us talk awhile. But mind you come alone. That other one is not welcome here.'

All knew that he meant Taliesin, and the Bard by way of answer made a mocking obeisance.

By skilful use of oars and rudder *Prydwen* was guided close to the base of the great rock, and there Arthur leapt lightly ashore. Scrambling, not without difficulty, on the slippery surface, he climbed swiftly to where the lone figure waited. There they spoke for a while, and none knew what passed between them, nor if the King struck some dread bargain with the Lord of Annwn. The warriors fingered their swords uneasily, ready if need be to leap ashore after the King and defend him to the last.

But soon they saw the King returning, and brought the ship close in enough for him to leap aboard. He seemed pale and shaken, and went straight to the prow and spoke briefly with Taliesin. None could hear their words, but the Bard could be seen to nod and smile his strange unchancy smile. Then Arthur gave the order to put out from the dreadful rock and back towards the centre of the natural bay formed by the surrounding basalt pillars. There the King ordered them to cease rowing and to look down into the water. They did so with no little fear, wondering what

further terrors that place held. What they saw has grown with the telling, and there are those who would dispute it. I can only tell what I was told, by one who was there on that day.

Looking down into the depths the King and his followers saw that the water had grown clear – so clear that as they stood upon the decks of *Prydwen* it seemed that they were flying above a vast land with nothing between them and it. Many cried out and clung to the sides of the ship for fear of falling. Below them they saw what seemed a vast city, spread out upon the sea's base. A city with buildings and streets and houses, where men and women walked in the pallid light of great milky stones which served as sun and moon in that place. And it is said that those below looked up and smiled and raised their hands in greeting to those above, and that some among them were the warriors who had but lately fallen or been consumed by the great serpent.

Then Arthur spoke aloud: 'Behold, the Cauldron of Annwn, on which we are permitted to gaze by its master. Let no one forget what he has seen today, for this is a great mystery.'

Indeed, none would ever forget that place, or what they saw, for each one it seemed saw something there which was for him alone, and there was little talking among the crew who survived on their voyage back to the lands of the living. Taliesin made his greatest song of it, and made of it a triumph, yet I cannot forget its refrain: 'Except seven, none returned from Annwn's Cauldron'.* While as to Arthur himself, who can say what passed between him and the Lord of Annwn? Was it this which kept him, while his warriors raised their cups in honour of the voyage, from drinking with them? I know not – only that it is said that on that day he first learned the true meaning of sovereignty.

And as to my Lord Taliesin, why, it was he who first told this tale, and who was witness to all that I have told. Let he who doubts any of it, take up the matter with him.

---

*Clearly the story-teller remembers another version of the poem to that which has survived (ed.).

·3·

Arthur and the Grail: The Medieval Vision

 ITH THE ENDING of the Arthurian era Britain returned to a state of darkness and confusion which was to last for several generations. Many of the native peoples fled across the Channel to Brittany and from there into Gaul and the Frankish kingdoms. Like many other such refugees, they took little with them in the way of goods. However, what they did take were their stories – stories, that is, of the old Celtic heroes, of the wonder-working cauldrons of the gods and of a new and recent hero: Arthur.

All of these tales went into the melting pot of the continental folk-tradition. Brittany itself had a largely Celtic community and was famed for its minstrels and story-tellers. It was here that stories of Arthur's disappearance rather than death began to emerge. It was said that he had not died but had been taken away to the mysterious island of Avalon, where he was destined to be healed of his wounds and then await the call to return and help his beleaguered people. From this beginning the extraordinary phenomenon of Arthurian literature was born.

THE HISTORY OF THE BRITONS

WHEN THE NORMANS conquered Britain in 1066 they brought their own minstrels and story-tellers, many of whom were of Breton origin, and with them came the stories of the 'old times' of Arthur and his heroes. In the five centuries between the exile of the Britons and the beginning of Norman rule the stories had undergone much augmentation. They now not only possessed a powerful Otherworldly quality but also bore the stamp of Frankish interests – including the still new concept of chivalry, the precepts of which governed the behaviour of the knightly class.

One man helped to bind the threads of tradition and history together,

ALBANY

Edinburgh

Caledonian
Forest

Hadrian's Wall

Carlisle

NORTHUMBERLAND

York

Humber

ANGLESEY

Wirral

Holy Head

St Asaph

Chester

Lincoln

Mount
Snowdon

(LOGRES)

WALES
(CAMBRIA)

Mount Pumlumon

Severn

Carmarthen

Brecon

Wye

Gloucester

St David's

Usk

Caerleon

Oxford

Milford Haven

Bristol

Swindon

London

Thanet

Bath

Thames

Sandwich

Glastonbury

Amesbury

Silchester

Canterbury

Cadbury

Salisbury

Winchester

KENT

Dover

Southampton

Tintagel

Camel

Totnes

CORNWALL

Barfleur

Rouen

Bayeux

NORMANDY

Mont
St Michel

Forest of
Broceliande

BRITTANY (ARMORICA)

A map of Arthurian Britain in medieval times, including some of the place names found in the works of Geoffrey of Monmouth and Thomas Malory uniting for all time the magical tales of Arthur and his heroes with the uncertain and fragmentary remains of early British history. This man was a cleric of Breton origin brought up in Wales. The name by which he was known was Gaufridus Monemutensis or Geoffrey of Monmouth, and his book, *Historia Regum Britanniae* (*History of the Kings of Britain*) appeared round about 1136. It was written in Latin, the language of the Church and the nobility, and it told the history of Britain from its 'settlement' by Brutus of Troy, through 1500 years of history, to the times immediately following the reign of Arthur.

Geoffrey claimed that the original source of his work was a certain 'very old book in the British tongue' which had been shown to him by Archdeacon Walter of Oxford, where Geoffrey lived between 1129 and 1151. The existence of this book has been challenged by historians of the period ever since. No trace of it has ever been discovered and it is generally considered to be a typical medieval apology, intended to disguise the true authorship of the work. Whether or not one accepts this premiss – and there is no more evidence for the book's non-existence than there is for its existence – the most important fact is that it gave historical credence to the age of Arthur. Even if the mysterious book never existed, it is certain that Geoffrey had access to many of the traditions and oral tales then circulating, several of which he will have heard in his native Brittany and others in his adopted Wales.

Though probably basing his work on earlier, historical texts, Geoffrey's tone is very different. The history is laced liberally with magic and wonders, and the intent is as much to entertain as to instruct. Perhaps for this reason the *Historia* became an instant success. Literally hundreds of manuscript copies were produced in succeeding years, making Geoffrey's book a best-seller in medieval terms.

The greater part of the book is given over to the Arthurian period, and establishes Arthur as a medieval king ruling over a court based firmly in the style and fashion of the twelfth rather than the sixth century. Thus when, after long struggles against rival factions, Arthur is finally made king, he invites kings, princes and archbishops from all over the land to a great celebration at the City of the Legions (possibly Chester). The scene is described in brilliant detail:

When they had all taken their seats according to precedence, Caius the server, in rich robes of ermine, with a thousand young noblemen, all in like manner clothed in ermine, served up the dishes. From another part, Bedver the butler was followed with the same number of attendants, in various habits, who waited with all kinds of cups and drinking vessels. In the queen's place were innumerable waiters, dressed with a variety of ornaments, all performing their respective offices . . . for at that time Britain had arrived at such a pitch of grandeur, that in abundance of riches, luxury of ornaments, and politeness of inhabitants, it far sur-

To King Arthur, Morgan le Fay reveals Lancelot's bewitched drawings of his love for Guinevere in this picture by Christian Loring

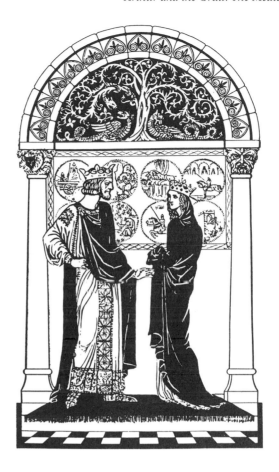

passed all other kingdoms. The knights in it that were famous for feats of chivalry wore their clothes and arms all of the same colour and fashion; and the women also no less celebrated for their wit wore all the same kind of apparel; and esteemed none worth of their love but such as had given proof of their valour in three several battles.

(Giles)

This was a far cry indeed from the more primitive picture presented in the fragmentary Celtic texts. It looked forward to the splendours of the medieval cycles which were to come in the next 300 years.

THE COMING OF MERLIN

THE BEGINNING OF Geoffrey's story takes place much earlier, and it has since been taken up and immortalized by dozens of writers. We are back in the time of Vortigern and his unsuccessful attempt to make allies of the Saxons, as told by Nennius, Gildas and other chroniclers of the Arthurian period. Just as in these sources, Vortigern is described as a most unpopular king who has attained his place by treachery and is eventually displaced, fleeing for his life into the mountain fastness of Wales. There he attempts to build a castle on a hilltop in the region of Snowdon. However, every night, when his masons have succeeded in building walls to the height of a man, these are thrown down by an unseen agency. Vortigern consults his Druids, who tell him that only the blood of a child born without a father, sprinkled over the foundations, will enable the walls to stand. Vortigern at once sends his soldiers out in search of such a child. In the nearby town of Carmarthen they overhear some children fighting in the street. One is taunting another, accusing him of having no father. The soldiers inquire in the town and learn that the child, whose name is Merlin, is the son of a local noblewoman who now lives in a nunnery. His father is unknown. The soldiers take both the child and his mother back to Vortigern, who questions the woman. She replies:

> 'My sovereign lord . . . by the life of your soul and mine, I know nobody that begot him of me. Only this I know, that as I was once with my companions in our chambers, there appeared to me a person in the shape of a most beautiful young man, who often embraced me eagerly in his arms, and kissed me; and when he had stayed a little time, he vanished suddenly out of my sight. But many times after this he would talk with me when I sat alone, without making any visible appearance. When he had a long time haunted me in this manner, he at last lay with me several times in the shape of a man, and left me with child.'
>
> (Giles)

Convinced by this recital that the child is indeed the one of whom his Druids have spoken, Vortigern is prepared to sacrifice him. But at this moment Merlin himself speaks up, challenging both the king and his advisers:

> 'Because you are ignorant [of] what it is that hinders the foundation of the tower, you have recommended the shedding of my blood for cement to it, as if that would presently make it stand. But tell me now, what is there under the foundation? For something there is that will not suffer it to stand.'
>
> (Giles)

The Druids are, of course, unable to answer and Merlin requests that a hole be dug, beneath which will be found a pool of water. This is done and the child is proved right. He then requests that the pool be drained, foretelling that beneath it will be found two hollowed-out stones containing a red and a white dragon. Again this proves correct, and at this juncture the two dragons rise into the air and begin a furious combat. The white dragon

Cadbury Castle, Somerset, long believed to be the original site of King Arthur's fabled city of Camelot (*John Rogers*)

is at first victorious, but the red returns to the fray with renewed strength and at last overcomes the white. Merlin, watching all of this, then begins to utter a long sequence of prophecies, starting with the meaning of the battling dragons:

'Woe to the red dragon, for his banishment hasteneth on. His lurking holes shall be seized by the white dragon, which signifies the Saxons whom you invited over; but the red denotes the British nation, which shall be oppressed by the white. . . . At last the oppressed shall prevail, and oppose the cruelty of foreigners. For a boar of Cornwall shall give his assistance, and trample their necks under his feet. The islands of the ocean shall be subject to his power, and he shall possess the forests of Gaul. The house of Romulus shall dread his courage, and his end shall be doubtful. He shall be celebrated in the mouths of the poeple; and his exploits shall be food to those that relate them.'

(Giles)

Never were truer words spoken, for of course the boar of Cornwall is Arthur, whose deeds and exploits must have most certainly kept many a story-teller in bread and butter up to our own time. Merlin's prophecies continue for many more pages, extending even to the very end of time itself, described in apocalyptic language.

The source for these prophecies is uncertain. Geoffrey almost certainly drew upon a number of oral traditions here, as with much of his work. He may also have had access to written material which has since perished. Whatever the truth, the prophecies of Merlin became so popular that separate editions of them were produced both shortly after and over several succeeding generations, and Geoffrey also produced a second successful book, the *Vita Merlini* or *Life of Merlin* (Parry). Although this had few specific Arthurian references, it none the less gave a powerful and convincing history to the famous magician and prophet.

THE BIRTH OF ARTHUR

RETURNING TO THE *Historia*, Merlin's prophetic outburst ends with the promise of Vortigern's own impending death and the return of two rightful claimants to the throne: Uther and Ambrosius, the latter recognizable as the same Ambrosius Aurelianus, 'last of the Romans', whose virtues and strengths as a leader were extolled by Nennius, Gildas and Bede (see Chapter 1). Here Geoffrey also makes Ambrosius fulfil the function of restorer of the flagging strength of the Britons, though only briefly, since he is keen to pass on to Vortigern's successor, Uther Pendragon, and to *his* son, Arthur.

Ambrosius is poisoned by a treacherous follower of the Saxons and, as he lies dead, a portent is seen in the skies over Britain:

> There appeared a star of wonderful magnitude and brightness, darting forth a ray, at the end of which was a globe of fire in the form of a dragon, out of whose mouth issued forth two rays; one of which seemed to stretch itself beyond the extent of Gaul, the other towards the Irish Sea, and ended in seven lesser rays.
>
> (Giles)

Uther is now crowned, taking as his title 'Pendragon' – that is, 'head' or 'chief' dragon – and adopting a banner of silk on which the great and terrible beast is depicted. His success against the Saxons is considerable and he

Camelot by William Ernest Chapman

The Round Table by William
Ernest Chapman

single-handedly welds the Britons into a fighting force and something of a
nation again. To mark this, Uther commands a celebration in London to
which the greatest in the land are bidden. Here fate takes a hand.

> Among the rest was present Gorlois, Duke of Cornwall, with his wife
> Igerna, the greatest beauty in all Britain. No sooner had the king cast his
> eyes upon her amongst the rest of the ladies, than he fell passionately in
> love with her, and little regarding the rest, made her the subject of all his
> thoughts. She was the only lady he continually served with fresh dishes,
> and to whom he sent golden cups by his confidants; on her he bestowed
> all his smiles, and to her addressed all his discourse.
>
> (Giles)

Of course, Gorlois can scarcely help but notice this attention and,
quickly sensing in what direction it is leading, he quits the celebration in
anger, taking Igerna with him. Uther, driven half mad with desire and
rage, pursues him with an army and lays siege to the castle of Dimilioc,
where the Duke has taken refuge, having bestowed Igerna in another
castle, Tintagel, perched high on the cliffs above the Atlantic.

There follows one of the most celebrated stories of the whole Arthurian
cycle. Merlin, summoned by Uther, agrees to help him. Using arts 'then
unknown in that time', he transforms Uther and his two henchmen into
the likeness of Gorlois and his captains. The three approach the gates of
Tintagel and are admitted. Uther lies with Igerna, who thinks him to be her
lord. Meanwhile, Gorlois himself issues forth in a sortie from his castle and
is slain - reputedly moments before Uther sires a child upon Igerna.

With the death of Gorlois Uther marries Igerna and in due course she
produces a son, who is named Arthur and is acknowledged as the rightful
heir to the King. Fifteen years pass and the Saxons begin attacking again.
Despite a debilitating illness, Uther is carried into battle on a horse litter
and from here he directs the proceedings, winning another victory. Shortly
after, he is poisoned and, as the country begins rapidly to fall apart, the
nobility request that the Archbishop crown Arthur as their new King.

THE HIGH KING

THE NEWLY CROWNED KING begins his own campaign against the Saxons. At first he has less success than his father or uncle, but with the assistance of 15,000 men sent by Hoel, the King of Brittany, the tide begins to turn. Finally, a great battle is fought. Arthur is described as

> having put on a coat of mail suitable to the grandeur of so great a king, placed a golden helmet upon his head, on which was engraved the figure of a dragon; and on his shoulders he carried his shield called Prydwen, upon which the figure of the blessed Mary, mother of God, was painted, in order to put him frequently in mind of her. Then, girding on his sword Caliburn, which was an excellent sword made in the Isle of Avallon, he graced his right hand with his lance, named Ron, which was hard, broad and fit for slaughter.

> (Giles)

In the ensuing battle Arthur displays such courage and strength that all honour him. In one rush, with Caliburn in his hand, he personally accounts for 470 men. Seeing this, the Saxons flee, and from this point the struggle is virtually over. In rapid succession, Arthur subdues the Picts and the Scots and then, carried on the tide of victory, adds the lands of Ireland, Iceland, Gothland and the Orkneys to his own. Soon after he further subdues Norway, Dacia, Aquitaine and Gaul, where he encounters the Roman consul Frollo, whom he defeats and slays. After this he returns to Britain and holds his coronation, as described above. At this same celebration he marries Guanhumara, better known as Guinevere, who is destined to become one of the most famous characters in the literature of the West.

At this point Geoffrey has given Arthur a family, an auspicious and mysterious birth, and a spectacular career of military victories. He has made Tintagel famous as the birthplace of Arthur (it had hitherto had no association with the story). Echoes of earlier tales abound in the details of Arthur's regalia and weapons – all of them surely derived from Celtic sources (note that the ship *Prydwen*, immortalized in the *Raid on Annwn*, has now become Arthur's shield Prydwen). Caliburn, later to be known by the name Excalibur, is the young hero's sword, crafted in Avalon. Now Geoffrey goes even further, extending the young king's conquests until news of them reaches the ears of Rome itself.

While Arthur is at Winchester, celebrating his victories, there comes a messenger bearing a letter from 'Lucius Tiberius, Procurator of the Commonwealth, to Arthur, king of Britain, according to his desert'. It begins:

> The insolence of your tyranny is what fills me with the highest admiration, and the injuries you have done to Rome still increase my wonder.

Glastonbury Abbey: now only a ruin, this was once the largest religious foundation in Britain; after it was partially destroyed by fire in 1185 the monks 'discovered' the grave of Arthur beneath the ancient graveyard (*Tim Cann*)

But it is provoking to reflect, that you are grown so much above yourself, as wilfully to avoid seeing this: nor do you consider what it is to have offended by unjust deeds a senate, to whom you cannot be ignorant the whole world owes vassalage.

After continuing in this style for several more paragraphs, the letter ends:

I command you to appear at Rome before the middle of August the next year, there to make satisfaction to your masters, and undergo such sentence as they shall in justice pass upon you. Which if you refuse to do I shall come to you, and endeavour to recover it with my sword, what you in your madness have robbed us of.

(Giles)

The response of Arthur and his captains to this is immediate. Cador, the fiery Duke of Cornwall, comments that he had been afraid the Britons would fall into a state of cowardice from the long period of peace to which they looked forward under Arthur, and that this would be a good opportunity to restore their military virtues! The other leaders being of a similar disposition, Arthur leads a huge army into Europe, leaving his nephew Mordred in charge of the country. A long account of the campaign now ensues, detailing attacks and counter-attacks, strategies, single combats and, finally, Arthur's overwhelming defeat of the Romans. Two heroes, Hoel and Walgan, save Arthur himself. The prominence of the former betrays Geoffrey's Breton sympathies (Hoel being a well known Breton hero), while Walgan is better known as Gawain.

All these detailed accounts of the campaign are, of course, completely fictitious. They may well be based upon earlier accounts of Magnus Maximus, a British general who, in 383, was proclaimed Emperor by his own troops and led an assault which, despite division among his followers and eventual treachery, took Maximus almost to the gates of Rome. In a similar fashion, it is treachery and betrayal which now bring about the downfall of Arthur. News comes from Britain that Mordred has proclaimed himself King and married Arthur's Queen, Guanhumara.

Geoffrey continues:

Of the matter now to be treated of . . . Geoffrey of Monmouth shall be silent; but will, nevertheless . . . briefly relate what he found in the British book above mentioned, and heard from that most learned historian, Walter, Archdeacon of Oxford, concerning the wars which this renowned king, upon his return to Britain . . . waged against his nephew.

(Giles)

Mordred, following in the footsteps of Vortigern, has made an alliance with the Saxons, even enlisting the help of those ancient enemies of Britain, the Picts and Scots. In the ensuing conflict, the day goes hard for Arthur, who loses many of his most loyal followers. However, finally the tide turns and Mordred, suffering a great defeat, flees to Cornwall, where, at a river named Cambula, a final battle takes place. In this many are slain on either side and, in Geoffrey's own words:

Even the renowned King Arthur himself was mortally wounded; and being carried thence to the Isle of Avallon to be cured of his wounds, he gave up the crown of Britain to his kinsman Constantine, the son of Cador, Duke of Cornwall, in the five hundred and forty-second year of our Lord's incarnation.

(Giles)

APOTHEOSIS OF THE LEGEND

GEOFFREY'S NARRATIVE continues for another eighteen chapters, dealing mostly with the struggles of Constantine and his successors with the sons of Mordred and their Saxon allies. The latter are never wholly

These medieval tiles from Chertsey Abbey depict scenes from the life of the Cornish hero, Tristan. On the left, he plays the harp to his uncle, King Mark of Cornwall, with whose wife, Iseult, he was soon to elope. On the right, Tristan is shown adrift in a boat

beaten, as they had been in the time of Arthur, and in the end, as predicted long before by Merlin, Britain falls under their yoke. Finally, the *Historia* draws to an end with the following statement:

> As for the kings that have succeeded . . . in Wales since that time, I leave the history of them to Caradoc of Llancarven, my contemporary; as I do also the kings of the Saxons to William of Malmesbury and Henry of Huntingdon. But I advise them to be silent concerning the kings of the Britons, since they have not that book written in the British tongue . . . which being a true history, published in honour of those princes, I have thus taken care to translate.

> (Giles)

Thus ends Geoffrey's extraordinary narrative. Both of the historians mentioned in this closing paragraph existed, and seem to have taken Geoffrey's advice to heart, since neither makes any significant mention of Arthur, beyond a few bare facts. They were probably right to ignore the fantastic story told by their Breton colleague, which certainly bears very little resemblance to history. However, whether he invented most of the saga of Arthur or took it from the now lost 'British book' is largely immaterial to the consideration of Arthurian history. Geoffrey's book was taken as literally true by his contemporaries (with the exception of a few who dismissed it as rubbish) and became the foundation upon which most of the succeeding generations based their ever-expanding tales of Arthur and his knights. Geoffrey's swift-paced, well-written narrative not only gave a coherent framework to the legends but also fleshed them out with names and characters who were destined to live on. Arthur himself, Merlin, Gawain (Walgan), Mordred and Guinevere (Guanhumara) were established as central characters in the web of Arthurian history and romance. Here is the famous last battle, mentioned by Nennius and now expanded into a fully fledged account by Geoffrey. Here too is the war with Rome, which in the hands of later chroniclers was to become a major theme in the burgeoning cycle.

It was all there, from Arthur's wondrous birth to his mysterious end. Heroic deeds, passionate love, panoply and splendour – all of it cast in the style and fashion of twelfth-century England. From here on there was no stemming the tide of Arthurian tales which began to appear, until the names and histories of the central characters were known the length and breadth of the Western world. Geoffrey spawned several imitators, who, in 'translating' his book into the languages of Norman France and Saxony, added significant details.

The first of these was Robert Wace, a Norman born in Jersey around 1100, who translated and adapted Geoffrey's book, concentrating solely on the Arthurian parts and adding the first known mention of the Round Table, at which Arthur's men met to tell of their adventures. His text is terse and gritty, full of the clangour of battle. No less important is the work of his follower Layamon or Lawman, of whom virtually nothing is known save that he was alive towards the end of the twelfth century and was English by birth. His book, *The Brut* – so called after Brutus, the supposed founder of Britain – put the stories into the language of the Saxon people and in so doing made Arthur an English hero. As the introduction to the 1962 edition, by Gwyn Jones, says:

Layamon was an intensely English poet. His subject was British history; his hero of heroes a British king who banged the English up hill and down dale and hammered the Alemain race from Iceland to Lombardy; his source book was Norman French; but his spirit, mood and manner were English. . . . Even the British Arthur becomes an Englishman, a Germanic hero, brave, daring and open-handed. We are in a world of feasts and vaunting speeches, flightings and lusty battles, fierce deeds and bloody humour . . .

As virtually every succeeding writer was to do from here onward, Layamon expanded upon his original, adding details to the history of the Round Table and gifting Arthur with Otherworldly ancestry. In describing his birth, Layamon says:

The time came that was chosen, then was Arthur born. So soon as he came on earth, elves took him; they enchanted the child with magic most strong, they gave him might to be the best of all knights; they gave

Sir Lanval by Thomas Bewick. In the story of Sir Lanval, or Launfal, the young knight marries a faery woman who later challenges Guinevere for the title of the most beautiful woman at Arthur's Court

him another thing, that he should be a rich king; they gave him the third, that he should live long; they gave to him the princely virtues most good, so that he was most generous of all men alive. This the elves gave him, and thus the child thrived.

Though we have come far from the Arthur of history, and despite the echoes of *Beowulf* and *Brunanburgh*, there is still a ring of the old Celtic stories about this. And when it comes to the description of Arthur's passing, Layamon gives him the following speech:

'I will fare to Avalun, to the fairest of all maidens, to Argante the queen, an elf most fair, and she shall make my wounds all sound; make me all whole with healing draughts. And afterwards I shall come again to my kingdom, and dwell with the Britons with mickly joy.'

As these words are uttered a boat appears on which are two women, the fairest ever seen. They take Arthur aboard and bear him away. And though no more is known of Arthur, Layamon tells us that the sage Merlin has foretold 'that an Arthur should yet come to help the English'.

With this, much of the saga is now complete. Arthur's birth, deeds and passing are known and fixed in all but detail. The most renowned of his followers are named, their deeds beginning to be chronicled as the fame of their king spreads wide. Argante, the mysterious lady of Avalon, will be encountered again many times over in different guise. Only one thread waited to be drawn into the pattern. It had been associated with Arthur in the earliest Celtic tales of the quest for a mysterious vessel. But Arthur himself was too revered, too great and noble a king, to embark personally on such a task. It now passed to another to become the destined seeker, and the story had already been told in the rich and magical tale of *Peredur mab Efrawg*, which we examined in Chapter 2. But this was too pagan in flavour to be associated with the great Christian King Arthur. A new flavour and a new direction were required, and emerged in the shape of a poem from the pen of an author who had already added significantly to the cycle of tales which began to surround the figure of Arthur. The author was Chrétien de Troyes, and the work was *Perceval, or The Story of the Grail*. We must turn now to this to see the next strand in the weaving of the great tapestry.

THE COMING OF THE GRAIL

CHRÉTIEN WAS BORN *c.*1135 at Troyes in Champagne and *c.*1164 became a poet at the cultured and sophisticated court of Countess Marie de Champagne, the daughter of Louis VII of France and Eleanor of Aquitaine. Apart from *Perceval*, he composed no fewer than five other Arthurian romances, including *Lancelot, or The Knight of the Cart*, in which the great French hero was introduced for the first time into the cycle in the guise in which he is most generally known, as the lover of Guinevere and the greatest knight in the world. Chrétien is also credited with writing the earliest surviving Arthurian romance, *Erec and Enide*, between 1167 and 1170. *Perceval* was, in fact, his last work, and when he began it, around 1185, he was already a mature and successful writer with a number of literary successes behind him.

In general terms, *Perceval* follows the story of *Peredur*, which we examined in Chapter 2, but Chrétien's version is a very different work from its Celtic relative. Witty, urbane and mystical by turns, it epitomizes all the qualities of the twelfth-century French romance. Its hero is seen as a foolish foil to the bright, worldly and sophisticated knights of Arthur's court, and his quest is no longer one of vengeance but concerns a mysterious object which is – at least on the surface – as far from the bloody head in the dish as it is possible to get. Gone are the nine hags, the serpents and the magic ring. Instead there are courtly scenes, urbane exchanges between the characters and references to a wider worldscape than the author of *Peredur* could have known.

There has been much speculation about Chrétien's sources. It has been pointed out that he seems to have had knowledge of at least one written and one oral version of a story in which a young knight visited the mysterious Grail Castle and failed to ask the all-important question concerning the Wounded King (see below). Whether the hero of this was in fact Perceval, or whether Chrétien married the basic story with an older Celtic tale of the kind found in *Peredur* is not certain. Whatever his immediate sources were, though – and they could have simply been oral tales heard in the court of his patron, Marie de Champagne, from travelling singers – Chrétien stamped the tale for ever with his own particular gifts as a story-

Balin and Balan by Louis Rhead. The brothers slew each other while wearing borrowed armour and weapons; only in death were they united

teller. Certainly he knew a version of Geoffrey's book, possibly in the version written by Wace.

The beginning of the tale follows *Peredur* closely. Perceval is brought up in the forest by his mother, who is determined that he will never know the ways of warfare and chivalry. However, the youth meets three of Arthur's knights in the forest and is determined to follow them. Again, we have the meeting with the Maiden of the Tent, Perceval's arrival at the court, Kay's insulting behaviour and the quest to discover the Red Knight who had thrown wine into the Queen's lap. Again Perceval blunders about until he is taken in hand by an older knight, here named Gornemant of Gohort, who is not related to him as in the Welsh version, but who gives him the same advice: not to talk too much or to ask impertinent questions. In a new episode Perceval defends a maiden named Blanchflor, with whom he spends an innocent night and is deeply in love.

The next day Perceval continues on his way, intending to return home and make peace with his mother, whom he had so wounded by leaving her to set out on his adventures. As he rides he comes to a river which appears to have no place to cross.

He rode along the bank until he came near a rock, and the river washed all round it so that he could go no further. But suddenly he noticed a boat with two men on board, sailing downstream. He stopped and waited, thinking that they would sail on down to him. But they stopped and stayed dead still in midstream, most securely anchored. The one at the front was fishing with a line, baiting his hook with a little fish slightly bigger than a minnow.

(Chrétien, 1982)

Perceval asks how he may find a way across the river and is told there is no way for many miles. However, there is a castle nearby where he may find rest and shelter. Perceval makes his way to a sheltered valley where there is a most beautiful house. He is welcomed there by its lord, a grey-haired man who suffers from an unspecified disability which makes him unable to stand or walk. While they are talking, a girl enters carrying a fine sword which has been sent to the lord by his niece. It is said to be the last of its kind, made by a swordsmith who is soon to die. The lord immediately bestows it upon Perceval, declaring that it is his destiny to bear it. While they are talking a boy comes from a chamber bearing a white lance which he holds by the middle of the shaft. A drop of blood runs down from the head to the boy's hand. Amazed, Perceval longs to ask what this means, but is mindful of Gornemant's instructions about asking questions and so keeps silent.

Just then two other boys appeared, and in their hands they held candle-sticks of the finest gold, inlaid with black enamel. . . . In each candlestick burned ten candles at the very least. A girl who came in with the boys, fair and comely and beautifully adorned, was holding a grail between her hands. When she entered holding the grail, so brilliant a light appeared that the candles lost their brightness like the stars or the moon when the sun rises. After her came another girl, holding a silver trencher. The grail, which went ahead, was made of fine pure gold; and in it were set precious stones of many kinds, the richest and most precious in the earth or in the sea: those in the grail surpassed all other jewels.

(Chrétien, 1982)

As with the spear, the grail is borne past the crippled lord and into an inner room. As before, Perceval fails to ask the meaning of these things.

Thus the Grail (with a small 'g') makes its quiet entry upon the Arthurian stage. It is not described further, and at this point possesses none of the miraculous qualities it was to gather around itself in the next few years. Indeed, nothing more is said at this time. Perceval and the crippled lord sit down to dinner and afterwards the young knight retires to bed. Next morning Perceval finds the castle strangely empty, and when he rides

Wearyall Hill, Glastonbury, Somerset: here Joseph of Arimathea arrived in Britain and planted his staff, which then burst into flower (*Tim Cann*)

out in search of his host or his men, the gate closes behind him and no one answers his calls.

A little further along the way he meets his cousin, who, again as in *Peredur*, is mourning her slain lover. In the ensuing dialogue she reveals that Perceval's mother has died of grief, and that his 'sin' had prevented him from asking two important questions: why does the lance bleed and whom does the Grail serve? If he had done so, the crippled lord would have been healed and disaster averted.

The story now follows the pattern of *Peredur* closely: Perceval avenges his cousin on the Proud Knight of the Tent, is found contemplating the blood in the snow, avenges himself on Sir Kay and, prompted by the castigation of the Hideous Maiden, sets out to find the Court of the Fisher King (now revealed to be one and the same with the crippled lord) and ask the questions about the Grail and the lance.

Chrétien now turns his attention to Gawain, who is described as Arthur's nephew and the best knight in the world. A series of adventures, perhaps designed as a foil to Perceval's, now follows. We then return briefly to Perceval, learning that he has wandered for five years in the wilderness, until he meets a hermit who is also his uncle, who explains that the Grail was serving the Fisher King's father, a man of such great spiritual attainment that he had been kept alive for years by means of a wafer brought to him daily in the Grail. The vessel itself he declared to be a holy object but would say no more than this.

Finally the story returns again to the continuing adventures of Gawain and ends, mid-sentence, as he prepares to undertake an important combat.

On the face of it, *Perceval* is a puzzling work which can have made sense only if the story were already a familiar one. We are told very little indeed about the Grail, and the motivation for Perceval's quest is far from clear. Why the Fisher King's father came to be kept alive by a single wafer, or the meaning of the spear that drips blood, or for that matter the nature of the Fisher King's disability – all are largely unexplained. This, together with the fact that the poem is unfinished – Chrétien apparently died before he could complete it – must have made it an intriguing puzzle. At any rate, no less than three people attempted to resolve the issue, extending the poem to more than three times its original length and, in fact, making matters less clear than before. The *'Elucidation'* which we examined in Chapter 2, was in fact supposed to be a prelude to *Perceval*, though it will be seen that the two stories have almost nothing in common and do not link up at all.

NEW DIMENSIONS

IF WE LOOK BRIEFLY at the continuations to *Perceval*, in which three very different authors attempted to write a successful conclusion to Chrétien's puzzling romance, we learn a few more facts about the mysterious Grail procession and the strange events which surround it, and perceive also a new dimension entering and changing the central myth of the Grail.

The first continuation is by a poet named Gautier de Danans, of whom nothing more is known. He takes up the story exactly where Chrétien left it, with further adventures of Gawain, which bring him at last to the Grail Castle itself. Here Gawain sees a room in which lies the body of a man holding a cross and broken sword – presumably the same inner chamber glimpsed by Perceval. Gawain is later presented with this and invited to restore it, which he cannot do. He is then declared unfit to achieve the mysteries of the Grail. In the evening he dines with the Fisher King and witnesses the strange procession. Mindful of Perceval's experience, he asks the meaning of these things, and learns that the spear was that which pierced the side of Christ as he hung upon the Cross. At this point he falls suddenly asleep and therefore fails to hear the rest of the explanation. When he wakes, he finds himself lying on the shore of the sea, while the land around him, which had hitherto appeared barren and wasted, has been restored to flower. A voice tells him that had he remained awake and succeeded in restoring the broken sword, all the ills of the Fisher King and his lands would have been healed.

Gautier now returns to Perceval and relates a series of adventures in

Arthur preparing for the war
against Rome, after a
fourteenth-century text of
Lancelot du Lac

which the young knight arrives at a castle which appears to be deserted
and in which is a wondrous chessboard set up for a game. When Perceval
sits down at the board, the pieces move of their own accord and easily
defeat him. Furious, he is about to fling the chessboard out of the window
when a beautiful faery woman rises from the moat and calls to him. He
immediately falls in love with her, but she refuses to have anything more
to do with him unless he brings her the head of a stag which is running
wild in a nearby forest.

The object of this seems merely to get Perceval into the forest, where he
sees a great light shining far off which is then extinguished. He encounters
a damsel who tells him it was the light of the Grail which had been given
to the world when Christ hung upon the Cross. After yet more adventures,
Perceval at last arrives again at the Grail Castle. As he once again witnesses
the mysterious procession, he does ask the required question, but instead
of this bringing about the profound revelations expected, he is told that he
must first mend the broken sword. In this he is successful, but Gautier
breaks off before the mystery can be explained.

In this text we see the first signs of a general trend which was to increase
with almost every telling of the Grail story. Somehow, the Grail and the
spear have become associated with the story of the crucifixion. Whether
this happened before Chrétien's telling and he simply chose to ignore it, or
whether it came about after the appearance of *Perceval* is impossible to say
with certainty. It seems likely, however, that at some point the stories of
the wonder-working relics of the crucifixion, which had certainly been in
circulation for several decades, were seen as the true source of the Grail
story. This is not surprising, since most of the story-tellers who expanded
upon the original tales were either Christian monks or clerics in holy
orders.

King Arthur riding with some of his knights, after a fourteenth-century text of *Lancelot du Lac*

Chrétien certainly made no such association, yet by the time Gautier's text appeared – no more than ten years after *Perceval* – the link was firmly established. The Grail is clearly associated with the Christian mystery, while the spear has become that which pierced the side of the Saviour on the Cross.

Yet even at this point the influence of older stories, probably Celtic in origin, was still felt. The entire episode of the broken sword which the hero is required to mend before he can achieve the rest of the Grail mysteries harks back to the episode in *Peredur* when the hero is required to cut through an iron pillar which then restores itself. These references are very much in line with other such tests undergone by heroes in which a sword either breaks at a significant moment or must be found and restored before they can be considered to have succeeded in their particular quest or adventure.

The second of the continuations, attributed to an author who goes simply by the name Menassier, extends the Christian symbolism even further and brings the poem to something like a satisfactory conclusion. In this Perceval returns to the court of the Fisher King and learns that the lance had belonged to the centurion Longinus, who in Christian myth is reputed to be responsible for the death-dealing blow to the Messiah. We then learn how Joseph of Arimathea, who in biblical tradition gives up his own tomb to contain the body of Christ, obtained the spear, while the Grail itself is the vessel in which he caught some precious drops of Christ's blood while preparing his body for burial.

Perceval then learns that the broken sword was that which had caused the Fisher King to be crippled, and that it can in fact be restored only when the evil knight responsible both for this wound and also the death of the King's brother is brought to justice and his head displayed on the wall of the Grail Castle.

Thus informed, Perceval sets forth and, after a goodly number of adventures, finally succeeds in avenging the murder of the Fisher King's brother. In due time he succeeds to the kingdom of the Grail, over which he rules for a further seven years. At this point an ancient hermit appears and leads him back into the forest, taking the Grail, the spear and the platter with him. There Perceval lives for a further ten years as a hermit himself, and on his death the relics vanish, believed, it is said, to have been carried directly to heaven.

Thus ends Menassier's attempt to conclude the story left unfinished by Chrétien. It is probable that he obtained most of his information regarding the history of Joseph and the Grail from another text, *Joseph of Arimathea*, by Robert de Borron (Goodrich), which had appeared some twenty years earlier. This gave a much fuller account of Joseph's acquiring of the Grail and the lance, and of his subsequent travels with a little group of disciples, in search of 'The Vale of Avaron', where the Grail would at last find rest. Here also the Grail is specifically identified as the cup used by Christ to celebrate the Last Supper – so that it is doubly hallowed by its further use as a container for some of the Messiah's holy blood.

In this same text we find reference to Joseph's brother, Brons, who receives the name of 'The Rich Fisherman' after he feeds the company of the Grail from a single fish – a clear enough reference to the miracle of the loaves and fishes from biblical tradition. Interestingly, of course, Brons is a name which derives from Bran, who, as we saw in Chapter 1, possessed a vessel of plenty and was also wounded in the thigh by a spear, receiving thereby a wound which would not heal. Even here, then, we can perceive echoes of Celtic tradition, which continued to influence the Grail story even after it had been Christianized. It is not even stretching matters too far to see, in the story of Bran, whose followers behead him after he receives the poisoned wound, the whole starting point for the wounded-king theme and even the head-in-the-dish story found in *Peredur*. Also, it is not too difficult to see a further echo in the recurring vengeance theme to be found in Menassier's story.

At this point, the interweaving of the texts is so complex as to virtually defy untangling. The number of inconsistencies and contradictions grows with each succeeding version. Nearly every text which appeared between Chrétien's *Perceval* in *c*. 1180 and the *'Elucidation'* in 1315 owes something either to its forebears or to Celtic tradition.

THE GREAT QUEST

THE THIRD AND FINAL continuation, which seems to have been composed at roughly the same time as Menassier's, is attributed to one Gerbert de Monteille. He was presumably unaware of Menassier's work, since he provides an alternative ending to the story. Here Perceval is reunited with his first love, Blanchflor, who bears him a son, Lohengrin, the Swan Knight, who founds a whole dynasty of Grail knights. (The great German composer Richard Wagner was later to write an opera based on this character in which he wove together not only the legends of the Grail but also the traditions surrounding the Duchy of Brabant, which claimed descent from Perceval and Blanchflor.) Gerbert's only other significant contribution to the story – now extended beyond the scope of any one story-teller – was to conclude the story of the broken sword, which is eventually restored by Perceval, who takes it to the smith who had forged it, at a place guarded by twin serpents. These Perceval must slay before he can reach the smith, who informs him that the sword was broken at the gates of paradise.

With these works the way was prepared for the great cycles of tales concerning Arthur and the Grail which were soon to appear. After Geoffrey of Monmouth's monumental work, which brought Arthur firmly into the medieval age, Chrétien's poem, and the works of Gautier, Menassier and Gerbert, bound the two great threads of the story indissolubly together. From now on there would continue to be a scattering of Arthurian tales, featuring one or other of the knights in search of adventure, but few major stories would be written which did not deal, in some way or other, with the Grail quest. The greatest developments were still ahead: the full flowering of the mysteries in texts which reflected the hunger for spiritual absolutes dominating the medieval world. The themes of human love and adventure continued to develop alongside those of the great search for the divine, but even these took second place beside the greatest of all stories: the quest for the Holy Grail.

Thomas and the Book

THIS STORY is based upon an episode from the thirteenth-century text of Perlesvaus. I have chosen to retell it in this form to give as strong an impression as possible of the man who wrote this extraordinary and visionary tale. It is also intended to show that the journey to discover one's own heart's ease is not necessarily a long one, as Thomas discovers here.

IN THE MIDST OF DARKNESS, as the weight of the night lay upon him with all its depths and mystery, Thomas became aware of light dim at first, but growing to such strength that he was almost unable to bear it. He sat up with a stifled cry, shading his eyes against the fierce burning in the night. And lo, the light spake! With each word or syllable turning and flickering as though to a harmony of sound and light.

'Thomas, know you who it is who speaks to you?'

'I know not.'

'I am the Master of masters, the one of whom it was said, all Wisdom cometh.'

'Voice, I am filled with doubt.'

The Voice was silent, flickering strongly. Then it spoke again.

'I am come to set aside your doubts. I am come to teach you a great mystery that you may set it down in writing for others that come after. I am the Voice of Tradition.'

Thomas was silent in his turn, having nothing that he might say to express the wonder he felt. 'And indeed,' he thought, 'I do dream most deeply this night.' But the Voice seemed to hear even his thoughts for it said:

'You do not dream. Here is a Book which shall tell you how the line of which you come is part of the shape of Time and follows that shape truly.'

Thomas then found that he was holding a small Book in his hands, and that the light had gone as utterly as if it had never been and that he was indeed awake in his small stone cell with the hard cot beneath him. And a great feeling of misery overcame him as well as a deep curiosity so that he rose and found a lamp and struck a light and looked at what he held.

To many it would have seemed strange, a wonder in itself, for there were few enough such things in that time. But to Thomas it was a Book and like all books it consisted of many sheets of vellum bound in leather, clasped about with bands of metal. It was not an especially rich seeming book – he had seen richer – its binding was plain and the clasps which fastened it were neither of silver or gold. Like lead they seemed, dull and heavy.

Slowly and with the care of one used to handling precious objects, Thomas opened the clasps and turned back the cover. A faint scent, as of incense, rose from the pages, which seemed new and unread. He opened the first folio and stared at the letters without at first understanding them. All of his attention went to the initial letter, which was written after an earlier style that he himself used. He remembered its like from other books in the scriptorium of his monastery and was, for a moment, back there with Brother Blaise at his elbow, hearing the harsh old voice, critical as ever, finding fault with his latest efforts to form the letters – long before his efforts first met with silence – the greatest the praise that the old master could offer. . . . Thomas brought his mind back to the Book in his hands and to the picture within the balanced uprights of the first letter.

Like a window into another world it showed a forest scene with a clearing in which was a fountain. Every detail of the ornate carving around its base was pictured there so clearly that Thomas could read every mark; and where the water fell in a silvered rain from the fountain he could almost hear the splash of the drops in the marble coping . . . with an effort Thomas brought his attention to bear on the words. He read:

'Here is the Book of Thy Lineage.

Here begin the Terrors.

Here begin the Marvels . . . '

He read no further but closed the book with a sharp snap that echoed in the confined space of his cell. A terrible panic had seized him. He trembled through his whole body and such a dread was upon him that for a long time he could neither move nor speak. Then at last he said, into the darkness beyond the flickering rushlight: 'Do I indeed dream?'

No voice came back from the corners of the room, but Thomas needed none for he knew that he was indeed awake. And then a weariness fell upon him that was as heavy as had been the fear of moments before, and without thought he put out the light and lay down, placing the little Book underneath his head, from where he drew in a fading breath of incense with his last waking thought.

Habit woke him and he was halfway to his knees with the first words of prayer upon his lips before he remembered the events of the night. He forced himself to remain awhile with eyes closed until he had completed *Ave* and *Paternoster*, only then opening his lids a crack and turning his head towards the bed . . .

He had been so certain that the Book would be gone, that when it was truly no longer there it took him several moments to realize. The shock brought him fully to his senses and he stared at the place where he had slept, recalling again the details of the night and the words of the Voice. Had he, then, dreamed in truth? Bending closer to the bed he saw that, impressed faintly into the thin mattress, was a shape – not the shape of his own head, but a small, square indentation. Again it was a moment before he understood: the Book *had* been real, his dream true. But (the thoughts coming faster now) if so then where . . . and how . . . and better still, why? Thomas sank back upon his heels and closed his eyes. Like a dim echo of the Light he saw a shining there, and like a faint, scarce-heard echo of the Voice, he heard words that told him what he must do, and how and when. But still they did not tell him why.

Next morning, Thomas rose early, and with an assurance born of inward certainty, set forth on the road. He went West, walking, taking nothing with him except enough food and water for a day's travelling. Long before that day was over he reached a meeting-place of four ways and there was a cross there. At its foot knelt a strange beast which was like no other that had ever been seen. It had the head of a sheep, whiter than snow, and its feet were those of a dog. Between these two points there was the body of a wolf that yet had the tail of a lion. And it was able to go upright upon its hind legs like a man, as Thomas discovered when it rose up before him. And he looked at the Beast and the Beast looked at him, and then it turned itself about and set off leading, and Thomas followed.

All through that afternoon the Beast kept up the pace, and Thomas went with it, following as he had been told to follow, without fear. As evening drew upon them the companions came to a deep, still valley surrounded by tree-lined slopes, and in the centre was a house that had lights shining in its windows. And Thomas was very glad to see that sight and hurried to the door which stood open.

There stood a man in the habit of a monk and he had a wise face and clear bright eyes. He welcomed Thomas and led him inside to where a table was laid with supper and he bade Thomas to say the words of blessing.

Of the Beast there was no sign, but the monk seemed not to know of it for he asked no questions. After he had eaten Thomas told of the reason for his journey and his host listened with bright eyes closed and said nothing until the end, when he looked straight at Thomas and said: 'This is a great thing which you seek; but a greater still is the mystery of your lineage, for you have heard the Voice of Tradition and all that is to be revealed is already within you.' But he would say no more though Thomas questioned him closely as to the meaning of his words.

In the morning Thomas and his host made their devotions together and then Thomas went upon his way with food and water enough for the second day of his journey. Nor was he surprised to find the Beast awaiting him upon the road, which they followed together as before until the midmost of the day, when they stopped to rest beneath a great tree that gave them shade from the heat of the sun. And as they sat thus a rider came in sight along the road, coming at a great pace. And when he saw where Thomas sat, with the Beast silent beside him, he reined in his mount and got down.

'Are you he who seeks the little Book?' he asked.

'I am indeed,' answered Thomas and he said again, eagerly, 'Have you news of it?'

'Not I,' said the stranger, 'but I am sent to bring you gifts,' and he gave Thomas a white cloth of very fine linen in which was wrapped a piece of cake and a little pot of tea and a cup from which to drink.

Thomas thanked the rider and asked who had sent these things.

'The Lady who lives within the Lake of Gold, hard by the Valley of Adventure.'

'Then may I come with you to this Lady, that I may thank her for this fare?'

'She bade me say that you have no need to thank her, but that you hasten onward and find that which you seek, for without you find it she may no longer stay by the Lake of Gold in the Valley of Adventure. And she bade me say also that she is of your lineage though you do not know her and that through you she shall continue.'

And so the messenger took his leave of Thomas, who was suddenly

aware that the Beast was gone before him again on the road, and he followed where it led, eagerly.

And so they went all the rest of that day until they came to a stretch of woodland that lay basking in the glint of the setting sun so that it seemed to glow from within, and there the Beast went apart amid the trees and Thomas found himself alone. Then ahead he saw a light and heard the sound of a voice upraised in a song of praise to the Most High. Hurrying forward he came to a clearing amid the trees and saw there a little chapel that lay almost hidden in a dip of the ground. It was from within that the voice came; high and clear-toned, exploring the shape of Heaven through its harmony of sounds.

Thomas stood as though spellbound until the Song was ended, only joining in the 'amen' which alone he recognized. At this there came forth from the chapel a strange figure dressed in rough-cured skins and carrying a long staff of oak in his hands with which he both supported himself and found his way. For Thomas saw that he was blind.

'Friend,' said the Singer (for so Thomas thought him), 'it is good that you have come at last.' Whereat Thomas was silent, for he knew with inward certainty that this man had indeed waited his coming for a long time, and that he, Thomas, had always known this, although until this moment it had not been in the forefront of his mind.

'Yes,' he said, softly, 'I have come indeed. Is what I seek here?'

'Not here; not yet; but not far. Come you within and rest and let he who accompanies you rest also –' by which Thomas knew that he referred to the Beast, and this was the first time that he realized that anyone but he could see the creature.

That night, as he lay upon the mattress of straw, scented with sweet herbs, Thomas thought that he dreamed. And in his dream came many people, some that he knew and others that he did not. And many of them were odd, curious people, who seemed not altogether of this world – beautiful women in dresses of green leaves, and fair tall men with shining stars upon their brows. And each one that came to him said: 'We are glad that you are seeking the Book, for within it are our lives and our being. And we are all of your lineage and you are the latest of our line.' And last of all came two figures who seemed older than all the rest, though in the prime of

their lives. They bore about them such a dignity that even in his dream Thomas felt the power and awe that surrounded them, and had he been in a waking state he felt that he would almost have fallen upon his knees before them. But they said: 'We are your Beginning and we are your End and in you is all that we are and all that we shall be, and upon you is the blessing of All Who are to Be.' And then they were gone and Thomas slept.

In the morning his host, the blind Singer, woke him and gave him fresh water to drink and set him upon his way through the wood, for of the Beast there was no sign. Thomas walked all morning among the trees, listening to the chorus of birds until he came at last to a clearing, in the midst of which was a fountain, which he recognized from the picture in the little Book. Upon it was written many things that he afterwards remembered only in odd moments, though from that moment his life was changed.

Then there came from the trees a fair young man clad in white and red, who carried in one hand an apple, and in the other the thing which Thomas sought. And he took the apple which was proffered first (not without a moment of doubt, remembering *another* apple) until he caught the merry eye of the youth and saw therein something that he recognized . . .

And when he had eaten the apple he saw that the wood seemed familiar and he remembered that it was near to his own small cell, whereat wonder fell upon him, for he had walked there often in the past but had never seen either the fountain or the young man. And as though he knew what Thomas thought, the youth smiled and said: 'It was always here, Thomas, though you saw it not. And I was always here also.'

Then he took up the little Book that Thomas sought and gave it to him. And Thomas took it with a trembling hand. But the young man only smiled and said: 'Go home, Thomas. Take pen and ink and copy out all that you find within this book that all who come thereafter may read it for themselves. And this you must complete in one year, and if you grow tired you shall come here to the fountain and take of its water and of the fruits that grow hereabouts. Do this in memory of all that have been and all that will be, for thus is the mystery of their lineage made plain for all who would see.' And Thomas bowed his head before the Voice of Tradition and when he raised it again he was alone.

·4·
The Great Flowering:
The High Books of the Grail

URING THE NEXT 100 YEARS the story of the Grail grew and developed beyond the wildest imaginings of the early story-tellers who had first shaped it. On to the scaffolding of Perceval's story was grafted a vast edifice of theological interpretation and commentary. Every nuance of the original story was examined, polished, changed and set in place, like jewels in a complex setting. New characters, including one who surpassed the original Grail winner and established a whole new branch of the mysteries, entered the story, which continued to expand with seemingly endless new adventures. Everyone, it seemed, wanted to know about Arthur and the Grail, and there was certainly no shortage of writers prepared to oblige.

Here we shall concentrate on just three of the major versions which have survived and are available in good modern translations.

THE MIGHTY DREAM

TO BEGIN WITH we must turn to a work which is now generally referred to as the *Vulgate Cycle* (Sommer), which is actually not one but five separate though interconnected tales which narrate the whole mighty saga of Arthur, from birth to death, and include the Grail story in magnificent detail. Once attributed to a cleric named Walter Map, the cycle is now seen as the work of several hands – probably monks and clerics of the Cistercian order, founded by Saint Bernard of Clairvaux in 1115. The cycle also marks the shift from tales composed largely in verse to those composed in prose. The resulting elaboration of theme and style makes for often heavy going, and the stories have a tendency to be almost lost under a welter of theology. Nevertheless, the *Vulgate Cycle* is in many ways a crowning achievement – the longest and most coherent of all the Arthurian romances. The five tales are titled as follows:

Estoire del Saint Graal (History of the Holy Grail)
Estoire de Merlin (History of Merlin)
Lancelot
Queste del Saint Graal (Quest for the Holy Grail)
Morte le Roi Artu (Death of King Arthur)

In terms of overall chronology, the first two romances are the *Estoire del Saint Graal* and the *Estoire de Merlin*, though both were in fact written after the other three. The first of these, the *Estoire del Saint Graal*, is little more than an elaboration of the *Joseph of Arimathea* attributed to Robert de Borron, mentioned in Chapter 3. It tells the story of Joseph and his descendants in highly religious terms, making them the essential repositories of the mystical Christian teachings and the guardians of the holy relics of the crucifixion.

An introduction states that the author, who wishes to remain anonymous, received a vision of Christ, who gave him a book containing the history of the Holy Grail. Basically, the story which follows is a thinly disguised excuse to explain the meaning of various doctrines – the Trinity, the Incarnation – in mystical terms. The focus of attention shifts rapidly from Joseph of Arimathea to his son Josephus and thence to a converted pagan prince named Nasciens. In a lengthy adventure, the latter finds himself on an island. A ship appears on which are a rich bed, a golden crown and sword of magnificient workmanship. Documents explain that these had once belonged to the biblical King David. On the bed were also three spindles of wood – one white, one red and one green. These were made from wood from the Tree of Life, which had begun as a white tree, turned red when Cain slew Abel and then green when Adam and Eve were cast out of the Garden of Eden. The ship had been constructed by Solomon and set adrift on the sea of space and time until it should become part of the Grail mysteries in the time of Arthur.

The story now turns to the arrival of Joseph of Arimathea and his little company in Britain, where they swiftly begin the task of converting the pagan inhabitants and founding various churches. Both Joseph and Josephus die, and a castle, called 'Corbenic', is built to house the holy relics. The line of the Grail kings is then described, various of them relatives of the later Arthurian characters – notably Lancelot and Gawain. One of the kings, Pelleam by name, receives a mysterious wound which will not heal, because of which he is called the 'Maimed King', and the area around the castle of the Grail becomes known as the Waste Land – a dead place where no water flows and no trees or crops grow.

In general, there is little new or significant in this romance. Its chief object was to set up a dynasty of Grail kings from whom many of the later Arthurian heroes could claim descent, and to set up the country of the Grail in preparation for the events which would be narrated in *Queste del Saint Graal*, volume four of the cycle.

THE LIFE OF MERLIN

THE SECOND VOLUME, *Estoire de Merlin*, draws upon a now-lost original, probably again by Robert de Borron, in which the history of the wise enchanter is given a biblical twist, and once again events are set in motion which prepare the way for the coming of Arthur. A long episode concerns the birth of Merlin, who is fathered by a demon as part of a plot to conceive an Antichrist who will combine spiritual and human qualities in the same way as the Messiah, but whose task would be the destruction of mankind rather than its salvation. However, the plan is frustrated by an observant priest, who baptizes the child. Merlin therefore retains his great powers but uses them for good. Shortly after this, Merlin seeks out a wise holy man named Blaise and dictates to him the story of Joseph of Arimathea and the Grail to date, along with a full account of his own strange engendering.

There follows a more or less straight retelling of the Vortigern episode, and of Uther's seduction of Ygene (Igerna). When Arthur is born, Merlin comes to claim him and carries him off into fosterage with a good man named Antor (Ector). The child is baptized Arthur.

In due time Uther dies and the kingdom falls prey to rival factions. Merlin, however, so orders things that the young Arthur arrives in London and there proves himself the rightful king in a famous episode in which he draws a sword from a stone which no one else can move.

Not everyone accepts Arthur's right to the crown, though, and there follows a long series of wars against rebellious lords and against the inevitable Saxons. In all of this Merlin proves a powerful guide, but he fails to warn Arthur against the wiles of his half-sister Morgause, upon whom he fathers a child, not knowing of their prohibitive blood relationship.

Further wars follow, with Arthur ever victorious. He subdues the rebel kings and then the Saxons, crowning his achievements by marrying Guinevere, the wisest and most beautiful woman in the land. Merlin, meanwhile, meets the beautiful Vivienne, a daughter of the goddess Diana. He is much attracted to her and displays his magical skills by summoning up fantastic troops of knights and ladies out of thin air. Delighted, Vivienne promises to love him if he will teach her more of his magic.

Arthur's war with Rome now ensues, much as in Geoffrey of Monmouth's account, save that Lucius has now become the Emperor rather than a simple Procurator. Arthur is victorious, however, and returns to Britain to learn that the Grail has been sighted. The chivalrous Order of the Round Table is now founded, with the knights swearing to right wrongs wherever they find them and to help all people in need.

Merlin now announces to Blaise and to Arthur that he must leave the world for ever. He plans to live with Vivienne in the magical forest of

A map of the mythical kingdom of Arthur as it appears in the great *Vulgate Cycle* of romances (after J. Neale Carmen)

Broceliande. Once there, however, she tricks him into revealing more of his magic and then entraps him under her enchantment. Gawain is the last person to hear Merlin's voice when he rides by the place where the enchanter is imprisoned.

With this the *Estoire de Merlin* ends. Like its predecessor, it draws heavily on earlier texts, in particular Geoffrey of Monmouth and Wace, but generally shapes events more coherently and lays the ground for what happens later. The episode in which Merlin is beguiled by Vivienne and later imprisoned has become one of the most famous and often retold stories in the whole mythos. Yet it is not what it seems. As I have shown elsewhere (J. Matthews, 1992), the story is a Christianized version of a much older tale, in which Merlin, growing weary of the world, retires to a magical observatory in the forest, where he is helped and protected by his sister Ganeida. Much of this story is preserved by Geoffrey of Monmouth in his *Life of Merlin* (Parry). By the time the French story was written, much of the original had been forgotten and it becomes instead an opportunity for the author to inveigh against the evils of women. Vivienne is henceforward portrayed as an evil enchantress, when once she was a wise seeress and prophet whose learning was as great as Merlin's own.

THE BEST KNIGHT IN THE WORLD

THE THIRD VOLUME now turns to the history of its greatest hero – Lancelot of the Lake. We learn that King Ban of Benwick, who has been a staunch supporter of Arthur throughout his wars against the rebels and the Saxons, had a son, who was first named Galahad and afterwards Lancelot. When the boy was still an infant, Claudas, an enemy of Ban, invades his kingdom and in the ensuing war Ban is killed. His queen, lamenting her husband's death and watching their castle go up in flames, lays her infant son on the earth for a few moments, only to see him carried off by a faery woman who lives beneath a lake. This was apparently the same woman who had imprisoned Merlin – the text summarizes this part of the tale, together with Merlin's birth, again.

Lancelot grows from child to youth in the magical house of the Lady of the Lake until, when he is fifteen, he is ready to go forth into the world. The Lady takes him to Arthur and personally asks the king to bestow the accolade of knighthood upon her young charge. Lancelot meets Guinevere for the first time and is innocently enraptured by her beauty. He embarks on a series of fantastic adventures and at length achieves the tests and trials of the castle named Dolorous Gard. He changes its name – to Joyous Gard – and makes the castle his home.

Lancelot now embarks on a further series of adventures; these take up

The Holy Grail by William
Ernest Chapman

several hundred pages in this immense work. As time passes he grows more and more hopelessly in love with Guinevere, who secretly returns his feelings. The two are at last able to declare their love through the machinations of a third party. At first their love is chaste, but when Arthur is briefly imprisoned by an enchantress named Camille, they become lovers.

Some time after this Lancelot happens by the Castle of the Grail and is made welcome. He succeeds in rescuing the Fisher King's daughter, Elaine, from an enchanted cauldron, and on the night following is tricked into believing that he is sleeping with Guinevere. In fact, he is in bed with Elaine, and on that night is begotten Galahad, of whom it is predicted that he will surpass his father and win the Grail.

Signs and portents begin to appear everywhere, and the mysteries of the Grail are approaching. Guinevere, learning of Lancelot's unwitting liaison with the Damsel of the Grail, upbraids him for his faithlessness to her. Lancelot goes mad as a result and wanders in the forest for many months, until he is finally rescued and healed by his cousin Bors.

At about this time Perceval, now fifteen, arrives at court and a hitherto mute damsel speaks and assigns him a seat at the Round Table next to the Perilous Seat – destined to be occupied by the Grail winner himself. The child Galahad is put to school in a convent governed by the Fisher King's sister. The romance ends with the announcement that the Grail will appear at the next Whitsuntide.

This immensely prolix work is a staggering achievement in story-telling. Written in a style known as *'entrelacement'* (interlacing), it keeps several stories – sometimes as many as eight – going at once, beginning one, bringing in a second, interrupting that with a third, and so on, eventually returning to the first. This method not only challenges the reader to keep a great deal of information in his or her head but also makes for a good deal of suspense – often the author will stop an adventure at a real cliffhanger, leaving the reader or listener to wait for fifty pages or so before the story is brought to a conclusion, or even interrupted again.

The story of Lancelot is really a long allegory about the strengths and weaknesses of chivalry. Lancelot is the strongest knight in the world but has a fatal flaw – he loves Arthur's queen. The outcome of this will be the eventual downfall of the Round Table and of Arthur's kingdom. At this point in the story the anonymous author brings off one of the most extraordinary episodes in the entire Arthurian corpus. He has Lancelot sleep with Elaine under the impression that he is in bed with the Queen. The outcome of this is the birth of Galahad, who will succeed in the Quest for the Grail. Thus out of the 'sinful' love of Lancelot and Guinevere comes the most perfect spiritual knight ever to sit at the Round Table. This is a masterstroke which could have been conceived only by a story-teller of the highest order. His skill changed the face of the story for ever.

Sir Galahad, Sir Percival and Sir Bors on the Last Ascent to the Castle of the Grail by Christian Loring

THE GLORIOUS QUEST

EVERYTHING IS NOW IN READINESS for the coming of the Grail and all the wondrous events which were to follow. With the beginning of the next book, *Queste del Saint Graal*, the carefully laid threads of the story begin to come together and the work moves towards its climax.

The story beings on Pentecost Eve and makes no reference to Galahad's conception. At Camelot, writing appears on the Round Table to denote

Sir Percevale of Wales by Walter Crane

each knight's destined place and announces that the 'Siege Perilous' will soon be filled. A floating stone appears in the river beside the palace, containing a sword destined to belong to the best knight. None is able to draw it out. During the meal, an ancient hermit enters, bringing Galahad. He announces that Galahad shall let loose the enchantments on the land. Galahad sits in Siege Perilous and his name appears on the table. He then pulls the sword from the floating stone and a maiden appears to gift him with a shield.

The Grail now appears, as the knights are seated at supper:

When they were all seated in silence, there was heard such a great and marvellous peal of thunder that it seemed to them the palace must collapse. But at once there shone upon them a ray of sunlight which made the palace seven-fold brighter than it was before. And straightway they were as if illumined with the grace of the Holy Spirit, and they began to look at one another; for they knew not whence this experience had befallen them. . . . Then . . . there entered in the Holy Grail covered with a white cloth; but no one was able to see who was carrying it. It entered by the great door of the hall, and as soon as it had come in, the hall was filled with odours as sweet as if all the spices of the earth were diffused there. And it passed down the middle of the hall and all around the high seats; and as it passed before the tables, they were straightway filled at each place with such viands as the occupant desired. When all were served the Holy Grail departed at once so that they knew not what had become of it nor did they see which way it went.

(Comfort)

Gawain vows to go in quest of the Grail and look upon its mystery openly. Everyone else promises to join the quest. Arthur declares this to be a 'mortal blow' to him personally, for he will lose his great Fellowship of Knights. The ladies wish to accompany the knights, but are forbidden by a hermit: 'For this is no search for earthly things, but a seeking out of the mysteries and hidden sweets of Our Lord.' Arthur bids farewell to his knights; Guinevere takes her leave of Lancelot. The knights go their separate ways.

The story now follows the adventures of each of the main knights, those of Galahad, Lancelot and Gawain taking up most of the space. Gawain encounters a hermit who tells him roundly that he will not succeed and explains graphically why: he is too much in love with the world, and beautiful women, to aspire to the heights of spiritual honour. Lancelot rests near a mysteriously deserted chapel where candles are yet burning and sees a sick man in a litter, though he does not greet him. The man laments that he shall never see the holy vessel. It appears on a silver table. The sick knight prays to it and is healed, but falls asleep instantly. The Grail returns to the chapel without Lancelot noticing. A squire returns to dress the healed knight and he brings him Lancelot's sword and helmet as well as his horse. Lancelot awakes as from a dream and enters the chapel to seek the Grail. He is told: 'Lancelot, harder than stone, more bitter than wood, more barren and bare than the fig tree, how . . . do you dare enter where the Grail is?' He laments and comes to a hermitage where he makes a confession. Able at last to unburden himself regarding his sinful love of Guinevere, Lancelot is absolved, and given new arms and rehorsed.

Perceval makes his way to the cell of an anchoress and finds that he is her nephew. She dissuades him from wanting to beat Galahad and tells him that he, Galahad, and Bors are destined to find the Grail. She explains that she was once Queen of the Waste Land and that his mother died of sorrow at his leaving. She also describes three great fellowships and tables – that of the Last Supper, that of the Holy Grail and that of the Round Table, instituted by Merlin.

'It was devised by Merlin to embody a very subtle meaning. For in its name it mirrors the roundness of the earth, the concentric spheres of the planets and of the elements in the firmament; and in these heavenly spheres we see the stars and many things besides whence it follows that the Round Table is a true epitome of the universe.'

(Matarasso)

Glastonbury Tor: here tradition has it that Joseph of Arimathea founded the first Christian church in Britain, and there housed the Grail (*John Rogers*)

As the Gospel was made manifest at Pentecost, so will be the Grail; the anchoress bids Perceval travel to Corbenic. As he journeys on, close to the sea, Perceval sees a boat coming towards him impelled as by the wind. The beautiful maiden of the boat tells him of Galahad's adventures and bids him accompany her. She sets up a tent to shelter them both, then feeds Perceval, who in turn woos her. As he is lying in bed, awaiting her, his gaze falls upon the red cross of his sword and the tent vanishes. Perceval wounds himself in the thigh in penance. A priest appears and prepares to lead him to Bors and Galahad.

Meanwhile, Gawain and his cousin Hector, with whom he has been travelling, are having an irritating lack of adventures. They both dream: Gawain of a field of bulls, Hector of Lancelot and himself stepping down from thrones and being refused a wedding feast. They wake and a mysterious hand holding a bridle appears through the door and a voice admonishes them. A hermit meets them and interprets their dreams. The bulls signify the pure and impure Grail knights. The throne of sovereignty signifies the relinquishing of Round Table prestige. The hand and bridle signify charity and abstinence.

The story now turns to Bors, Lancelot's cousin. He meets a maiden who desires him. When he repulses her, she threatens to leap with twelve of her maidens from the tower. Bors refuses her and she jumps. The tower and maidens disappear and fiendish shrieks are heard. Bors then hears a

voice which bids him seek the sea and Perceval. He finds a boat with white
sails in which is Perceval and they tell each other of their adventures.

While staying at a hermitage, Galahad is called to follow a maiden who
conducts him to the ship where Bors and Perceval are. The maiden says
she is Perceval's sister, Dindraine. They see a canopied bed with a crown
and a scabbardless sword upon it. Dindraine explains the sword: the ship
came to Logres in the time of Lambar, the father of the Maimed King, and
King Varlan the pagan, who drew this sword and used it to wound Lambar
the Christian. This was the dolorous blow. The sword belt proclaims that it
may not be unfastened save by the hand of a princess who will exchange it
for a worthy belt and the maiden shall truly name the sword. The framework over the bed is made of the white, red and green woods described in
Lancelot.

Dindraine weaves a belt from her hair and names the sword Memory of
Blood. Galahad takes it. They get into their own ship and sail onward.
Later they are stopped, Dindraine is captured and a leprous maiden seeks
to be healed by Dindraine's blood. After mass, Dindraine is bled, but the
bleeding will not stop and she starts to die. She bids Perceval and Galahad
put her in a boat and go to Sarras, where they will find her.

The Grail Appears to Lancelot
Sleeping by Walter Crane

Arthur is carried to the Otherworld in a boat filled with keening women. Charles Gere's wood engraving for Sir Thomas Malory's *Morte D'Arthur* (Ashendene Press, 1913)

AND THERE RECEYVED HYM THREE QUENES WYTH GRETE MOURNYNG, AND SOO THEY SETTE THEM DOUN, AND IN ONE OF THEIR LAPPES KYNG ARTHUR LAYD HYS HEED. AND SOO THAN THEY ROWED FROM THE LONDE.

Lancelot, meanwhile, still finds himself hemmed in by a dark forest, high rocks and deep rivers. He enters a boat without oar or sail, sleeps and on waking sees Dindraine's body. He reads the letter placed there by Perceval. At last he meets Galahad and they stay on board for six months. During this time they grow to know and love each other and share many adventures. Then, at Easter, they meet a hermit with a horse who bids Galahad carry on with his quest.

After a month alone at sea, Lancelot comes to a castle guarded by two lions. He draws his sword and is transfixed by a flaming hand. He enters the chapel of the Grail and rushes forward to help support the priest whom he perceives as holding up the body of a crucified man. He is paralysed and blinded for daring to enter the holy place. Slowly he is nursed back to health and finds that he is at Corbenic. Lancelot comes to a table which is set by the Grail but afterwards departs and returns to Camelot.

Galahad, Perceval and Bors wander for a further five years. They come to Corbenic and Pelles greets his grandson. The sword with which Joseph of Arimathea was wounded in the thigh and which is broken is brought in.

Galahad unites it and a voice bids all unclean persons avoid the hall. Some newcomers arrive from other countries and a bed is borne in by four maidens. All leave save the Grail companions. The Maimed King is on the bed. Josephus, the first bishop, mysteriously appears and the holy things manifest in the hall. Christ appears from the Grail and gives each of the knights to drink. Galahad anoints the Maimed King with blood from the lance, healing him. They find the Ship of Solomon again and now the Grail appears on it. They set sail and arrive at Sarras, and take the Grail and table into the city. Galahad is made King of Sarras. After a year celebrating mass, Galahad looks in the Grail and dies. Perceval and Bors see a hand snatch up the Grail to heaven. Perceval becomes a hermit and Bors stays for a year until Perceval dies. Bors then returns to Logres and tells Arthur all that has occurred.

Thus ends this great and magisterial account. Despite its great length, prolixity and extensive theological argument, it is a truly powerful and at times awe-inspiring romance. Few can fail to be moved by the story of Lancelot and his all-too-human struggle to overcome mortal love and achieve the spiritual mystery. Perceval and Bors seem shadowy by comparison, and certainly Perceval is a less important figure than Galahad. It is Lancelot's son who holds centre-stage throughout most of the romance, dominating it with his saintly presence. He has been described as a cold and bloodless hero, but in truth he is a simple and godly man who undertakes the task for which he has been born with strength and honour. The months he spends with his father in the Ship of Solomon are filled with moving moments as their relationship grows and develops. In the end both are ennobled – Lancelot by his son's extraordinary purity of mind, Galahad by his father's stubborn worldliness. When Sir Thomas Malory incorporated this part of the French romance into his great book *Morte D'Arthur*, he made it one of the most moving episodes in the entire book.

THE ENDING OF THE DREAM

THE FINAL BOOK in the sequence, *Morte le Roi Artu*, returns to the court of Arthur. Bors arrives back at the court with news of the deaths of Galahad and Perceval and the final achieving of the Grail. Lancelot and Gawain both return, though many do not. Lancelot soon forgets the promises he made during the quest and goes back to his adulterous relationship with the Queen. This is now suspected by several people, including Gawain's brother Agravain, who attempts to persuade Arthur of the lovers' crime. Arthur, however, refuses to believe it – even when Morgan le Fay shows him a series of murals painted by Lancelot which depict his love for Guinevere. But the whole of the Arthurian court is now feeling the effects

Gareth and Linet by Louis Rhead. The newly knighted Sir Gareth of Orkney rode on his first adventure accompanied by the sharp-tongued Linet; eventually she was forced to recognize his bravery after he had saved her from various dangers

of the quest. Mordred, Arthur's bastard son, has now appeared at the court, and begins stirring up trouble against his father. Many of the younger knights turn against the King and the old days of the Round Table Fellowship seem gone for ever.

Guinevere is accused of murdering the brother of Sir Mador de la Porte and, according to the law of the time, is given forty days to find a champion to defend her honour. Lancelot, who has been recovering from wounds received in a tournament, returns in the nick of time to save her. After the Queen's acquittal she and Lancelot become careless and soon even the loyal Gawain and his brothers are aware of what is going on. One day Arthur overhears them discussing the affair and demands to know all. Though still reluctant to believe the story, he agrees to go on a hunting expedition, leaving both Lancelot and Guinevere behind. Agravain, Mordred and Guerrehes hatch a plot and catch the lovers together in the Queen's chamber. But Lancelot's superior strength and skill carry all before him and he escapes. Guinevere is now arraigned and sentenced to death at the stake. Her guards include Gawain's youngest brother, Gaheriet, and when next day Lancelot and Bors (who had fled with him) return to rescue the Queen, Gaheriet is among those slain. This so angers Arthur that he closes the ports against Lancelot and Guinevere and lays siege to Joyous Gard.

Lancelot now offers to settle the quarrel by single combat and Gawain, angered at the death of his brother, takes up the challenge. The combatants are too evenly matched, however, and nothing is resolved. The siege drags on for a month until the Pope intervenes, instructing Arthur to take back his Queen and allow Lancelot to depart to his own country. To this Arthur

A contrite Guinevere prostrates herself before Arthur in this nineteenth-century engraving by Gustave Doré to illustrate Tennyson's poem *Guinevere* (1867)

agrees, but, egged on by Gawain, he follows his old ally across the sea and attacks him again, leaving Mordred in charge of the kingdom and the Queen.

Events move swiftly to their climax now. Lancelot and Gawain fight again and Lancelot wounds his old friend in the head. News comes of an approaching Roman army, and Arthur turns aside to defeat them. Word arrives of Mordred's treachery, and the Britons return home to fight a last battle. Gawain dies at Dover, after warning Arthur of Mordred's treacherous nature. Arthur has a dream in which he sees himself dashed down from fortune's wheel. The last battle takes place and in it Mordred is slain and Arthur mortally wounded. Of the Round Table Fellowship only Lucan, the butler, and a knight named Griflet survive. Lucan dies next day and Griflet helps Arthur to the seashore, where he throws Excalibur into the water. A hand rises from the water, catches it and brandishes it thrice before drawing it beneath the waves. A ship in which are Morgan le Fay and many other ladies arrives to take the King away. Griflet discovers his tomb next day and brings the news to Guinevere, who, having taken the veil of a nun, dies soon after. Lancelot, returning to Britain with an army, defeats Mordred's sons before himself retiring to a hermitage. There he dies soon after, leaving only Bors alive of all the old fellowship. He lives the rest of his days as a hermit and dies of sweet old age.

Thus ends this extraordinary saga of the birth, deeds and death of Arthur, his knights and their ladies. In 1480 an English knight named Sir Thomas Malory was to turn this vast cycle into one of the greatest books ever written in the English language, *Morte D'Arthur*. He cut the massive volumes by more than half, jettisoning the theological arguments and courtly descriptions, and replacing them with realistic dialogue and a fast-moving narrative style which make the book so much of a joy to read to this day. He also included the story of Tristan and Iseult, a pair of lovers as famous as Lancelot and Guinevere.

His book is memorable for many reasons: its sense of character, its style and the sheer gift of the story teller have seldom been equalled. Malory makes the Grail even more mysterious than it is in the *Vulgate*, explaining very little and embellishing so deftly that one is left gasping in admiration at his subtlety. The end is more open than in the French version. Arthur's death is obliquely reported and Malory comments:

> Some men say in many parts of England that King Arthur is not dead, but that by the will of our lord Jesu into another place; and men say that he shall come again. . . . I will not say it shall be so, but rather I will say: here in this world he changed his life.

The *Morte D'Arthur* could not have been written without the existence of the *Vulgate Cycle*, which is still the most complete retelling of the stories ever attempted. It may lack pace and characterization to our modern ears, but it more than makes up for this in the sheer inventiveness and richness of the stories, which tumble on, like a vast unstoppable river, for hundreds of pages. Copies and variants abounded as the Matter of Britain became the most popular story in the Western world. Arthur had come a long way from the writings of Geoffrey of Monmouth, though it is still possible to see the skeleton of the *Historia* beneath the elaborations of the *Vulgate*.

THE PERFECT FOOL

WITH THE COMPLETION of the great cycle, it seemed there was no more that could be said on the subject of the Grail. Yet more was still to be written, including several works which are rightly judged among the great books of Western literature.

Perceval delivers a young lion from the serpent, after a drawing in the Biblioteca Nazionale, Florence (Cod. Pal. 556)

Of these, *Parzival* was composed by a Bavarian knight named Wolfram von Eschenbach *c.* 1207. As such it predates the composition of the *Vulgate Cycle* and looks to Chrétien's *Perceval* for its source. In fact, it tells much the same story as the French poem, but is vastly elaborated and threaded through with a huge and mysterious symbolic structure involving numerology and a precise organization of the chapters so that the story spirals inward to the centre (Chapter 24) and outward again to the end. Much ink has been spilled in attempts to crack Wolfram's 'code' and arrive at a deeper, more esoteric meaning within. If such a meaning exists, it is secondary to Wolfram's primary purpose – to tell a great story as well as he knows how, and to put right what he considers to have been the mistakes of Chrétien! At the end of the book he states that the French writer has done little justice to the story, which in truth originated with one Kyot of Provence. Nothing has ever been discovered about this mysterious figure, who is generally supposed not to have existed. This is merely a trend among current scholarship, which believes that if no other mention of a source or author exists, it must therefore be an invention. There is really no reason why this should be so, or indeed why Kyot should not have existed and have told a version of the Grail story which Wolfram heard and used as a basis for his own poem. Whatever the truth, *Parzival* makes fascinating reading.

It begins with a lengthy account of the hero's parents. Gahmuret, a knight of Anchou, meets Belcane, a Moorish queen, during a Crusade. He marries her and then departs for home, leaving her twelve weeks' pregnant, with a note to tell her of her son's ancestry. Gahmuret returns to Christendom and fights in a tournament called by the Queen of Waleis, Herzeloyde, who offers herself and two kingdoms for the prize. Gahmuret

defeats everyone in sight and wins Herzeloyde. He admits his love of Belcane, but her heathen state is no obstruction to Christian marriage, says Herzeloyde. They are married.

While Gahmuret is absent at war, Herzeloyde has a vision of a shooting star which sweeps her into the air. A griffin snatches at her right hand; she gives birth to a serpent which rends her womb; a dragon suckles her breasts and disappears. She wakes and is told of Gahmuret's death. She is delivered of a large boy whom she names Parzival.

Herzeloyde now removes to the wildness of Soltane and there raises Parzival in the usual manner. The story follows closely on that of Chrétien, but with greater elaboration. When Parzival finally reaches the Grail Castle and witnesses the procession, he sees a bleeding lance borne by a youth, two maidens with candelabras, a duchess and her companion bearing trestles, four maidens with candles, four more bearing a garnet-hyacinth stone all dressed in green robes, two noblewomen bearing a pair of silver knives on napkins, four maidens bearing candles, six more maidens in cloth of gold, and finally the beautiful Repanse de Schuoy bearing the Grail.

> Her face shed such refulgence that all imagined it was sunrise. . . . Upon a green achmardi she bore the consummation of heart's desire, its root and blossoming – a thing called 'The Gral', paradisal, transcending all earthly perfection!

(Wolfram, 1980)

The 'Gral' gives every food that is desired and it is said that those who stand in its presence will never grow old. As in all the versions so far considered, Parzival fails to ask the question and next morning finds himself alone, except for a page, who berates him for failing to ask the Grail question. Eventually, after many adventures which parallel those of the other Perceval romances, the hero meets a company which inform him that it is Good Friday and reproach him for carrying arms on such a holy day. They take him to the cell of the hermit Trevrizent, where Parzival is told all about the Grail.

Here Wolfram breaks with his sources and embarks on an account of how Kyot the Provençal found the text in Toledo. It was apparently written by a mysterious figure named Flegetanis, a heathen astrologer who read the name of the Grail in the stars. He said of it that:

> A troop left it on earth and then rose above the stars. Whether or not their innocence drew them back again, a Christian progeny bred to a pure life had the duty of keeping it. Those humans who are summoned to the Gral are ever worthy.
>
> (Wolfram, 1980)

This intrigued Kyot so much that he embarked upon an extensive search through many books in Latin and other sources, finally composing the book upon which Wolfram himself is drawing for his story.

After hearing the history of mankind from the Fall to the present, including the stories of the Wounded King (here named Anfortas) and of the Family of the Grail, whose appointed task it is to guard the sacred object, Parzival prepares for the last part of his journey. On this he has to face the evil Klingsor, a castrated magician who seeks the Grail for himself to use its power for evil. Parzival, however, comes again to the castle of Anfortas and this time asks the question. He is proclaimed lord of the Grail and, amid general rejoicing, marries his great love, Condwiramors. At this point we are introduced to Feirefitz, a parti-coloured knight who is the offspring of the liaison between Parzival's father and the Moorish princess. As such he is Parzival's half-brother, and after some disagreement they are reconciled. Through the wondrous operations of the Grail, Feirefitz is baptized and marries Repanse de Schuoy, the Princess of the Grail. Their son is said to be Prester John, the mysterious Priest-King who rules over a far-off land away to the east.

This is all new material, and very fascinating reading it makes. Highly mystical, it takes the Grail story to new and different heights. Such details as the provision of Parzival with a parti-coloured half-Arabic brother who is seen to be as noble as any Christian knight were rare at the time when the poem was composed. Then the shadow of Islam lay over the whole of the Western world and all 'Saracens' were regarded as evil and potential enemies.

The revelation of the Holy Grail, after a drawing in the Biblioteca Nazionale, Florence (Cod. Pal. 556)

The characterization of Parzival himself – as 'the Perfect Fool', whose innocence enables him to survive the challenges of the quest without scathe – is perhaps the most subtle and wide-ranging of any of these texts, while the change of the Grail from a vessel to a stone is unusual also, and curiously seems to echo the wondrous stones of earlier Celtic sources. Wolfram also gives a considerable amount of space to the delineation of the Grail Family and their particular tasks as guardians of the sacred relic. We shall return to this in the final chapter.

The material dealing with the evil 'anti-Grail king', Klingsor, seems to hark back to the story of Amangons and the Damsels of the Wells (see Chapter 2), as well as to a mysterious 'invisible knight' named Garlon who appears in Malory's *Morte D'Arthur*. It is possible, indeed, that the names Amangons, Klingsor and Garlon derive from a single etymological stem. If this is the case, what we have is a kind of composite portrait of an anti-Grail king, a dark aspect of the actual guardian. In the case of Garlon, he is actually described as the brother of the Grail king, and there is a suggestion that the same relationship once existed between Klingsor and Anfortas. Amangons, though not related to Arthur by blood, functions as a kind of opposing force before the coming of Mordred later in the stories.

Each of these characters, then, is in some sense responsible for the advent of the Waste Land, which, from a purely localized event, becomes more widespread and generally felt in the later Arthurian texts. Thus, by the time we get to the thirteenth-century story of *Perlesvaus, or the High History of the Holy Grail* (Bryant, 1982), the failure at the heart of the Arthurian kingdom, which is illustrated by the Waste Land, has become more directly linked with the actions of Arthur himself, whose failure to take the initiative in the quest – leaving it to his knights instead – is seen as a failure of will and of his sovereignty.

In this sense the Waste Land has become indicative of a more general malaise – the heart of the kingdom, its king, is ailing, and until both are healed, by the finding of the Grail, the land will not be cured.

In his sometimes radical reshaping of the elements of the story written by Chrétien, Wolfram took the whole matter of the Grail into a new dimension, deepening and extending its range into a mysterious world of Templars, Eastern astrology and even black magic.

Arthur sets sail for Avalon, after a fourteenth-century drawing in the Bibliothèque Nationale, Paris

THE ENDLESS QUEST

IT WOULD BE POSSIBLE to extend this account of the Grail for many more pages, dealing with such wonderful texts as *Perlesvaus*, supposedly written at Glastonbury in the thirteenth century, or indeed the magical 'Didot' *Perceval* (so called after its first editor), which gives Merlin a far more prominent part to play in the ordering of the Grail quest (Skeels). But to do so would be both to duplicate what has gone before and to confuse the clear and overwhelming structure of the *Vulgate Cycle*, which above everything sets the Grail in its place within the Arthurian corpus and helps to define this mysterious object throughout the vast extent of the story.

The story does not end here, however, and in the final chapter we shall look at some of the ways in which the Arthurian and Grail mysteries have continued to fascinate and inspire into the present day and at some of the ways in which we, as students of those mysteries, or as followers of the endless quest, can ourselves become part of 'the Family of the Grail'.

Galahad and the Holy Things

PERHAPS the most perfect rendition of the Grail story is to be found in Sir Thomas Malory's great book Morte D'Arthur. *Here the author reduces the prolix and wandering account of the French* Vulgate Cycle *into a tight and powerful tale of mystical adventure, in which the strength of the human spirit is tested to the extreme. In the story which follows I have for the most part followed Malory, but I have set the rendition in the voice of the professional story-teller of a medieval court.*

———— ◆ ◆ ◆ ————

MY LORDS! You have heard the story of how the renowned King Arthur and his knights of the Round Table set forth in search of the Holy Grail, but the story I would tell you is of the noble knight Sire Galahad – how he fared upon the quest and how he met with his noble father Sire Lancelot, and how they sojourned together for many days in the magical Ship of Solomon. Thus my story begins, that is told for your good entertainment.

It was May-time when Galahad came, his red armour gleaming amid the bright blossoms like blood upon the petals of a rose. His coming was mysterious, ushered into the hall as the Round Table Fellowship sat at meat together by an old withered man who leaned upon a stout ash staff. Wonder was upon every face in that place of many wonders, as he silently led the beautiful youth to the Siege Perilous, that seat in which it was said no man might sit but the one appointed to achieve the greatest adventure of all – the finding of the Grail.

This alone spoke of strange and wondrous events. But while the knights fell silent, glancing towards each other and to where the King sat in his great chair at the Table with them, another and greater wonder befell. For there was a great crashing and crying elemental force, and all the wooden shutters banged shut, and the great doors to the hall were sealed so that none might enter or go out. Then a strong wind arose which blew throughout the hall and guttered all the candles. In the darkness there came a hush,

and then one of the windows flung open with a crash and into the dimness there shone a ray of light that was brighter by far than any candle flame. Within the ray all there espied a thing – a beauteous and radiant Cup which floated above their heads, emitting such power as none there had ever felt before.

Every man there began to look at his neighbour, and it is said that what they saw was the truth about each other, so that many dropped their gaze, or fell to looking again in awe at the bright wonder which floated serenely above them. Then the aged man, he who had guided the red-armed youth to his place, spoke up.

'Here begin the mysteries of the Grail. Now begins the time of testing and of sorrow. For many shall go forth this day, but few shall return and fewer still shall discover what they seek. This youth is named Galahad. I recommend him unto you all.'

As he spoke these words the light that shone from the Grail grew dim and then, my lords, it was no longer there. Light and movement returned to the hall of the Round Table, the doors and windows were unsealed, and men sat blinking in wonder at what had transpired. Some might even have believed themselves to have fallen asleep and to have dreamed the events, but that there sat the pale youth in his gleaming suit of iron-red mail, and that there was besides a sweet savour in the air as of summer flowers or the incense which scented the great basilica in the city below.

Then into the silence and uneasiness leapt the voice and figure of Sire Gawain.

'My lords and my friends, hear me! Such wonders as we have seen this day! Let all know that I make this vow, that I shall not rest nor cease from searching, until I have discovered the true meaning of these things.'

Many there murmured their ascent, while others sprang from their places and cried aloud that they too would set forth at once in search of the bright mystery. Only Arthur sat still and silent, sunk in thought. And when at last he spoke – all there turning at once to hear him – it was with heavy words.

'My lords, your courage and your ardour do you credit. Yet I fear that I shall not see many of you again, and that this may well be the ending of our great Fellowship. Yet I wish you well, and send you forth with my blessing.'

Having said which, the King arose and walked slowly from the hall,

leaving many to wonder at his words, while others sat still and thought upon their own mortality.

My lords, you know well what befell then. Within the week every one of the Fellowship then present had set forth, led by the boldly spoken Sire Gawain. They went by all the roads leading from the city and if at first they set forth with high hopes in goodly companies, they were soon silent and, as days turned to weeks, and one or another turned aside upon a different path, increasingly alone. The chronicle of their deeds has been told before, and will be told again. Many fell upon that quest who had lived and fought for the good of both land and king. Few were chosen to see or hear the great mysteries of the Grail. Gawain himself, who was ever light of purpose, soon turned aside to other things and the story tells of him no more. Instead, it speaks of four knights: Sire Perceval, Sire Bors, Sire Galahad and Sire Lancelot. These four came closer than all the rest to the heart of the Great Mystery, and each of their stories would take a night to tell. Here I would tell only of two: Sire Galahad and Sire Lancelot – of how they met upon the quest and of what transpired because of that meeting.

Lancelot had been long upon the road when he came one day to the shore of the sea and saw there a strange ship with silent red sails on which was emblazoned a bright picture – the Grail itself with a sunburst around it. In the boat sat a single figure, pale bright hair spilling over his travel-worn red clothes. At sight of the mail-clad figure on the shore, he lifted his hand in greeting and beckoned to Lancelot to join him. Recognizing the youth who had come on that fateful day and who had sat in the Siege Perilous unscathed, Lancelot dismounted and, leaving his horse to wander free, went aboard the strange ship. At once a wind sprang up and the sail filled, driving the craft from the shore and out on to the ocean.

Once Lancelot would have questioned a vessel which set forth without benefit of crew, but so many strange events had dogged his path since leaving Camelot that now he no longer even thought to ask. Instead he looked long and straight at his companion. And saw there himself mirrored.

'How is it that we are so alike?' he asked in puzzlement.

'Do you not know?' came the quiet answer.

And as Lancelot heard the words it seemed that he *did* know. His mind went back to a time, many years since, when he had rescued a girl from a bath of boiling water, whence she had been set by dire spells, and how that

same night he had received a message that seemed to come from the Queen, summoning him to her rooms in a nearby castle. How sweet that night had seemed – until, on waking, he had discovered the girl he had but lately rescued by his side.

His mind returned to the moment of that waking and then as swiftly back to the serious face of the youth before him.

'You are Elaine's child.'

'I am.'

'Then, you are my . . . son.'

A trembling began in Lancelot's limbs. It seemed impossible that he had not known it before, had not seen it writ large upon the boy's face that first time when he had entered the hall of the Round Table. Tears he had not known were in him clouded his eyes and he reached out blindly to Galahad.

If they two both wept that day I know it not, or will not speak of it. But it is certain that they had many things to say to each other as the mysterious ship drove on through the sea. Mayhap Galahad spoke of his childhood among the sisters of Amesbury, where his mother had sent him to learn the ways of prayer and of the Great Mystery he was destined to seek. For this had been his task from birth, and he knew of no other. As for Lancelot. whether he spoke of the love which tore at his very soul, I shall not say. Only that in the days which followed, the two men talked of many things, and they each found fellowship and love in the other.

Then, one night, Lancelot had a dream. He dreamed that he stood outside the door to a chapel from which radiant beams of light shone forth, and that as he looked within he saw an aged priest celebrating the Holy Mass. And as he came to the Offering of the Host. Lancelot thought that he struggled to hold aloft the body of a man, who bled from hands and feet and brows . . . and he rushed forward unthinking to help . . . and was struck down by a breath as of fire, while a Voice spoke in his head which said: 'Not for you the way of the Grail! You have chosen another path.'

Lancelot awoke with tears upon his cheeks and told Galahad of his dream. The young knight was silent for a long time, but at length he said: 'My noble father, I think you know the meaning of this dream. It is a thought which has been in my mind since we met upon this voyage and already it is a cause of great sorrow to me, though I know it must be so, and that there is no gainsaying the destiny that is laid upon us both. For I

Lancelot and Galahad

believe the time is fast approaching when our paths must take us on separate ways.'

As though his words had ushered in a change, the sails of the boat flapped and it turned about in the water, making for land. There, in the distance, but growing swiftly larger, was a castle set atop a cliff. Bright light came from it as though it were built of sun and air. Lancelot and Galahad looked upon it together and said nothing more to each other until the ship grounded upon the shore. Then Galahad rose and placed a hand upon each of his father's great shoulders and looked deep within his eyes.

'Though we meet never again in this world, yet am I glad that we have shared these days together.'

Lancelot smiled. 'It is small enough time for a father to know his son.'

Galahad smiled back, but said no more. And though he took leave of Lancelot with love and warmth, yet it seemed that his eyes ever turned towards the guiding star of the castle, and his thoughts were already upon the task which lay before him.

And so the two knights, father and son, parted. Nor did they indeed meet again in this life. Lancelot watched his only son walk alone up the path towards the castle, never once looking back, his whole soul intent upon the Great Mystery. Then, as he watched, the sails above his head filled again with the breath of the air, and the ship moved away from the shore. Lancelot's last glimpse was of the castle, shining like a star on the headland far above, and he heard a sound which seemed to him like the note of a great bell sounding forth into the dimming day.

That night he dreamed again, and the dream seemed to him a gift from the Cup of Love itself. For as he lay restless in the boat that carried him ever further from the place his heart longed to be, he saw again the chapel from which he had been turned away. And there he saw his son, clad now in raiment of white, holding before him a Great Spear, while before him stood One whose face was all of light, and who held the vessel of all heart's desire in his hands, and offered Galahad to drink. . . . With all his soul in his eyes the young knight took what he had sought from the day of his birth, and in his dream Lancelot could not bear to look upon the face of his son as he drew back and sank upon his knees, then slid slowly to the ground. Two other knights, whom Lancelot recognized as Perceval and Bors, held the body of their comrade and laid it down upon the floor of the chapel. Then a great pealing of bells and voices broke out, waking Lancelot from sleep.

In that moment it seemed that he could still hear the sound, which faded as he woke, cold and alone on the ship, his cheeks wet with his own salt tears.

Yet these were tears not of sorrow but of great gladness, for he felt the joy of his son's achievement as though he were there to speak of it in person. Even though Lancelot himself was destined to return to Camelot, and to turn again to the love which had become a canker in his soul, yet the bright blessing of the Great Mystery, perceived by him through the love of his son, was sufficient to awaken in him an answering joy. As he turned his mind towards Camelot and the Queen, his heart was light at last, and the memory of Galahad was bright within him.

·5·

Seed Bearers: The Family of the Grail

 LTHOUGH THE GRAIL and Arthur were considered unfashionable after the great works of the twelfth to fifteenth centuries, the myths did not die out. Instead, they took a new turn, a direction which led into strange waters – though no less fascinating and marvellous for that.

Running at times parallel to the written texts dealing with Arthur and the Grail, an ongoing oral tradition which drew upon folklore, ancient mystery teachings and so-called 'heretical' offshoots of Christianity continued to grow and put forth buds.

In fact, the seeds of this tradition were present in various of the texts already. Arthur was widely believed to be alive and well in Avalon, waiting the call to help his country, while the mystical nature of the Grail stories in particular prepared the way for an awakening interest in the teachings of earlier belief systems. What had once been perceived as a cycle of stories and legends took on a patina of mystical awareness. This led to a search for the inner meaning of the stories, and hints and clues were sought among the pages of the medieval manuscripts.

THE MYSTERIOUS QUEST

THERE WAS CERTAINLY no shortage of clues to deeper mysteries – those of the Grail in particular. What, after all, was this strange and mysterious object? We have seen it described as a cup, as a cauldron and as a stone. It is also said to have been the cup with which Jesus celebrated the Last Supper or in which Joseph of Arimathea caught some of Christ's blood as he washed the body in preparation for placing it in the tomb.

From the beginning it was a mysterious thing. Robert de Borron, writing *c.* 1212, had described the imprisonment of Joseph of Arimathea by the Romans. While in prison, Joseph received a visit from the risen Christ,

A wonderfully Victorian illustration, depicting Merlin – complete with coiled Druidic serpent – from Sir Walter Scott's semi-Arthurian poem *The Bride of Triermain* (1864)

King Arthur.

And so lovely seem'd she there,
Spell-bound in her ivory chair,
That her angry sire, repenting,
Craves stern Merlin for relenting ;
And the champions, for her sake,
Would again the contest wake,
Till in necromantic night
Gyneth vanish'd from their sight.

who not only gave the Grail into his keeping but instructed him in the mysteries of its use. However, these were not to be spoken of aloud or passed on to everyone, but were to be kept as part of the 'Secrets of the Saviour' and relayed only to those who formed the 'Family' of the Grail. Later, as Joseph is dying, the voice of the Holy Spirit speaks to him, telling him that he has established a lineage which will continue until, in a far-off time, one will come who shall achieve the Grail. This is Perceval, and a promise is made:

Then shall be accomplished and revealed the significance of the blessed Trinity which we have devised in three parts. . . . And when thou hast done this thou shalt depart from this world and enter into perfect joy which is My lot and the portion of all good men in life everlasting. Thou and the heirs of thy race . . . shall be saved . . . and shall be most loved and cherished, most honoured and feared of good folk and the people.

(Schlauch)

This alone would have made the Grail story a subject of speculation. With the added inconclusiveness of Chrétien's poem, the complexity of the three 'continuations' (see Chapter 3) and the increasing weight of theological commentary, the whole subject became surrounded by a veil of mystery.

AN INNER HISTORY

LOOKING AT THE SUBJECT TODAY, with a mixture of hindsight and the evidence of the texts themselves, it is possible to trace something of what might be termed the 'inner history' of the Grail. To begin with, its attributes help define it. In the *Queste del Saint Graal*, as the Grail appears for the first time before the assembled knights of Arthur's court, it dispenses the food most desired by each person. In the same romance, as in virtually every text we have looked at, it provides sustenance for the Wounded King. And it acts as a kind of testing device for the quest knights: only those who are spiritually worthy can be in its presence, as witnessed by what happens to Lancelot when he enters the Chapel of the Grail and tries to approach the mystic object.

Despite this – or because of it – many have sought their own path to the Grail. On the way, they have illumined many hidden corners of tradition and have laid down something like a history, which traces the holy relic on its long peregrination through time and space.

THE SECRET OF THE STONE

IN *Parzival* Wolfram tells us more of the mysterious Castle or Temple of the Grail and its guardians, the 'Templiesen' (Templars), a force of formidable fighting men whose task it is to guard the Grail. He goes on (the hermit Trevrizent is speaking):

'I will tell you how they are nourished. They live from a Stone whose essence is most pure. If you have never heard of it I shall name it for you

here. It is called "Lapsit exillis". By virtue of this Stone the Phoenix is burned to ashes, in which he is reborn – thus does the Phoenix moult its feathers! Which done, it shines dazzlingly bright and lovely as before! Further: however ill a mortal may be, from the day on which he sees the Stone he cannot die for that week. . . . For if anyone, maid or man, were to look at the Grail for two hundred years, you would have to admit that his colour was as fresh as his early prime, except that his hair would be grey! Such powers does the Stone confer on mortal men that their flesh and bones are soon made young again. The Stone is also called "The Gral".'

(Wolfram, 1982)

This is fairly unequivocal. The Grail confers extended life and vitality to all who are in its presence. But what are we to make of the strange words 'Lapsit exillis' or the mention of the phoenix? Both would seem to be references to the mysteries of alchemy, the medieval proto-science which sought both to prolong life and to transmute base metal into gold. 'Lapsit exillis' is a kind of Latin, but means nothing at all. It has been suggested either that it was an elaborate joke on Wolfram's part or that he had simply misheard or misunderstood the words 'lapis exilis', which mean small or slight stone. This may well be a reference to the 'lapis philosophorum' or philosopher's stone, sought by the alchemists as an important stage in the process known as the Great Work. Like the Grail itself, which transforms those who seek it spiritually, the Great Work was concerned with transformation – of metal into gold, of the spirit of the alchemist to a higher or more perfect state of being.

There is still another possibility, which leads us to a curious and fascinating answer. In *Parzival* the stone is green and has been brought to earth by a troop who left it on earth and rose high above the stars. What is this strange troop, and why were they bringing the Grail to earth? Wolfram gives an interesting answer, placed, as is so often the case, in the mouth of the wise hermit Trevrizent:

'When Lucifer and the Trinity began to war with each other, those who did not take sides, worthy, noble angels, had to descend to earth to that Stone which is forever incorruptible. I do not know whether God forgave them or damned them in the end: if it was His due He took them back. Since that time the Stone has been in the care of those whom God appointed to it and to whom He sent his angel. This, sir, is how matters stand regarding the Gral.'

(Wolfram, 1982)

Prester John and his page, from a nineteenth-century engraving. According to legend, John ruled over a vast Christian empire in the East; he is said to be the current guardian of the Grail

This, by any account, is extraordinary. What Wolfram is telling us is that the Grail, the most holy object ever to be found on this earth, was brought here by 'neutral' angels who refrained from taking sides in the heavenly war between God and Lucifer, the rebel angel of the Morning Star.

This is a far cry indeed from the version to be found in works like the *Vulgate Cycle* or *Perlesvaus*. It appears to directly contradict all the remaining Grail texts. Yet remember that the Stone itself is described as 'incorruptible'. It is a piece of the matter of heaven transported to earth. The circumstances of that transferral are less important. The whole Grail quest turns on this. For, if the Grail is truly a piece of heaven, or, as it is termed in Malory's version of the Grail story, 'the Spiritual Place', then the reason for the quest becomes clear.

Humanity, in its never-ending search for meaning, its desire to understand its place in the scheme of things, seeks ever to relate itself to a higher state of being. This is the reason why only those of pure intent can achieve its mysteries. This is why Klingsor, Garlon or Amangons, who each desire the sacred thing for the power they believe it can offer them, are bound to fail. The Grail cannot be owned by anyone.

THE FAMILY OF THE GRAIL

IT DOES, HOWEVER, possess its guardians, the mysterious Grail Family mentioned by Wolfram and others. In *Parzival* we are told something of their origins and purpose.

> Maidens are given away from the Gral openly, men in secret, in order to have progeny . . . in the hope that these children will return to serve the Grail and swell the ranks of its company. . . . As to those who are appointed to the Gral, hear how they are made known. Under the top of the Stone an inscription announces the name and lineage of the one summonee to make the glad journey. Whether it concern girls or boys, there is no need to erase their names, for as soon as a name has been read it vanishes from sight! Those who are now full-grown came here as children. Happy the mother of any child destined to serve here. . . . Such children are fetched from many countries and for ever after are immune from the shame of sin and have a rich reward in heaven.
>
> (Wolfram, 1982)

Wolfram here seems to be speaking of a physical succession, perhaps even of an élite body of people who are bred to serve the Grail in a wholly calculated way. He also indicates that the disposition of the Grail lineage is a secret known only to the angels. Earlier in the text, we remember, he had spoken of the troop of angels who left the Grail on the earth, 'a Christian progeny bred to pure life [who] had the duty of keeping it'.

Thus the Grail secrets are passed on, from father to son, up to the time of the great Arthurian quest. Before then it was kept in a hidden place, a

The Procession of the Grail

temple where it could be revered until such time as mankind was deemed ready to be told of its existence, shown its miraculous powers and offered the chance to go in search of what it represented.

THE TEMPLE OF THE GRAIL

DESCRIPTIONS OF THIS PLACE are found in several of the texts we examined in the previous chapter, and from the start certain features appeared fixed. The temple generally stood at the top of a mountain, surrounded by either an impenetrable forest or a stretch of wild water. Access, if any, was more often than not by way of a narrow bridge, which frequently had a sharp edge. From this it became known as the Sword Bridge and many knights come to grief trying to cross it. Sometimes, to make entrance even harder, the temple revolves rapidly.

One of the most detailed pictures of the Grail Temple appears in a thirteenth-century poem called 'The Later Titurel' (Wolfram, 1984), composed *c.* 1270 by a poet named Albrecht von Scharfenburg. He drew widely on Wolfram's *Parzifal* and devoted altogether 112 lines of his work to a description of the temple so specific in detail that is seems more like the description of an actual place than a poetic fancy.

Titurel, Parzival's grandfather, is fifty when an angel appears to him and announces that the rest of his life is to be dedicated to serving the Grail. He is then led into a wild forest from which rises a mountain called the Mountain of Salvation (Munsalvache). There he finds workers recruited from all over the world who are to help build a temple to house the Grail – which at this time floats in the air over the mountain, held there by angels. Titurel sets to work and levels the summit of the mountain. Soon after, he finds the ground plan of a building mysteriously engraved on the top. It is to take some thirty years to build, but during this time the Grail provides not only the substances from which the temple is to be built but also food for the workmen. At length it is complete and at this point we find the following description:

The Temple arose as a wide and high rotunda, bearing a great cupola. Twenty-two chapels stood out in octagonal form; over every pair of chapels stood an octagonal bell-tower, six storeys high. At the summit of each tower was a ruby surmounted by a cross of white crystal, to which a golden eagle was affixed. . . . In the middle of the roof arose a great central tower richly decorated by many goldsmiths. At its summit was a carbuncle, which shone forth at night. Should any Templar return late to the castle, its glow showed him the way . . . .

Two doors led into each of the chapels. Each one contained an altar of

View of Rosslyn Castle, as it was when perfect: according to local tradition, the Grail is hidden in the 'Prentice Pillar', a marvellously carved decoration within the present-day chapel of Rosslyn

sapphire, which was so placed that the priest should face to the east. The altars were richly decorated with pictures and statues; over each one a high ciborium. Curtains of green satin protected them from dust. . . . In the east stood the main chapel, twice as large as the others. It was dedicated to the Holy Spirit, who was the patron of the temple . . . .

On the wall between the chapels were golden trees with green foliage, their branches filled with birds. Golden-green vines hung down over the seats; roses, lilies and flowers of all colours could be seen. . . . Over the vines were angels, which seemed to have been brought from paradise. Whenever a breeze arose they came into movement like living beings.

The portals were richly decorated in pure gold and in every kind of precious stone which was used in building. . . . The windows were of beryl and crystal, and decorated with many precious stones, among them: sapphire, emerald, three shades of amethyst, topaz, garnet, white sardonyx and jasper in seventeen colours . . . .

The cupola rested on brazen pillars, into which many images were graven. It was decked with blue sapphire, on which stars of carbuncle shone forth both day and night. The golden sun and silver-white moon were pictured there . . . cymbals of gold announced the seven times of day. Statues of the four Evangelists were cast in pure gold, their wings spread out high and wide. An emerald formed the keystone of the cupola. On it a lamb was depicted, bearing the cross on a red banner.

In the midst of the temple was a rich work dedicated to God and the Grail. It was identical in form to the temple as a whole except that the chapels were without altars. In this the Grail was to be kept for all time.

(Meeks)

Here the magical vessel is kept, watched over by a select body of knights drawn from the Family of the Grail. Wolfram called them Templiesen

(Templars), and while it is possible that he means simply 'guardians of the temple' by this term, it is also possible that he is referring to an actual body of men, whose history is as much wrapped in mystery as is that of the Grail.

THE SOLDIERS OF GOD

IN 1118 a Burgundian knight named Hughes de Payens, together with eight companions, all Crusaders, founded a new order of chivalry, dedicated to poverty, chastity and obedience and established specifically to guard the pilgrim routes to the Holy Land. This was something quite new in the Western world, though similar orders existed in the East. The idea of combining the piety of a monastic way of life with the rules of chivalry must have seemed as startling as it was original. Yet little is known about the man who founded the order except that he described himself as 'a poor knight', and held a small fief at Payens, only a few miles from Troyes, where Chrétien was to write his Grail story some sixty-two years later.

The other significant fact about Hughes de Payens is that he was related to Bernard of Clairvaux, one of the most famous theologians of the age and the founder of the Cistercian order. It was to Bernard that Hughes now wrote, begging him to sponsor the new order and to give them a rule by which to direct their lives.

After some hesitation Bernard took up their cause, and it was largely due to his influence that the order was ratified at the Council of Troyes in 1128. They were permitted to wear a white robe with a red cross emblazoned on the right shoulder, and were given, as their headquarters in the East, the building believed to have been the Temple of Solomon in Jerusalem. From this they received the name by which they were ever after known – the Knights Templar.

From this beginning grew the single most famed military organization of the Middle Ages. The Templars became the permanent 'police' of the tiny war-torn kingdom of Jerusalem. They fought with utter dedication and became feared by Muslim and Christian alike. Bernard's rule was a harsh one, binding the knights to forswear home and country, to fight at need to the death and to neither ask for nor give any quarter.

Bernard's sponsorship was sufficient to swell the ranks at a rapid rate. Soon the order began to build a network of castles, called *'commanderies'*, across the Holy Land, as well as in France, England and elsewhere in Europe. Their power and strength increased, and their wealth grew accordingly. Though each individual renounced personal possessions, they gave freely of their goods to the order and also began to win much treasure in their battles with the Moors. In time they became so wealthy and of such good standing that they were virtually the bankers of Europe, lending

The St Michael Tower sits atop Glastonbury Tor like a beacon to all who pilgrimage to this magical place (*John Rogers*)

huge sums to help finance the Crusades. And, as their political power grew, so their enemies increased. Finally, the miserly and avaricious King of France, Philip the Fair, plotted with a renegade Templar to bring about their downfall – for the most astonishing of declared reasons.

Philip charged the order with heresy and in a single night had the greater part of their number taken prisoner. They were tortured and, under pressure, admitted to every kind of crime, from sodomy to spitting on the Cross. The last Grand Master of the Knights Templar, the saintly Jacques de Molay, was executed on 19 May 1314, bringing the order effectively to an end 196 years after its foundation.

Such are the historical facts. Behind them lies an even more remarkable story, which may well be closely linked to the inner history of the Grail.

There are several facts about the Templars which warrant notice. First, there is their name, which though said to refer to the Temple of Solomon is also reminiscent of the 'Templiesen' of Wolfram. Then there is the connection with Bernard of Clairvaux. As well as the Templar rule, he also composed his *Treatise in Praise of the New Order of Knighthood*, in which he speaks of the order in terms which are easily applied to the Grail knights:

It seems that a new knighthood has recently appeared on earth, and precisely in that part of it which the Orient from on high visited in the flesh. . . . It ceaselessly wages a twofold war both against flesh and blood and against the spiritual army of evil in the heavens.

The idea was something wholly new. Though the church had long seen itself as the army of God, this had never been taken to the extreme of actually arming its priests. The idea seemed a contradiction in terms. Yet this is precisely what the Templars became, priests and soldiers – 'doubly armed', writes Bernard, so that they 'need fear neither demons nor men'. He adds, 'These were the picked troops of God.'

Yet these men, who, as Bernard says, will be 'in the company of perfect men', are later reviled, their order discredited and destroyed. Why should this be so?

Among the crimes, both sacred and secular, of which the Templars were accused are listed the harbouring of the heretical group known as the Cathars and friendship with the Islamic sect of the Ismaelites – their nearest equivalent in the East. Both accusations are possibly true, at least in part.

The order did offer sanctuary to wrongdoers, provided they renounced their former lives and obeyed the Templar rule. The period of testing was lengthy, however, and discipline strict. It is also more than likely that certain Cathars, fleeing from persecution in the south, did find their way into the order and may even have influenced it from within.

As to the suggestion, made by several historians, that the Templars were friendly with the Islamic sect of the Ismaelites, this is also likely enough. Though the order began with the avowed intention of destroying the Infidel and of winning back the Holy Sepulchre permanently for the Church, constant encounters with the Arab way of life had a transforming effect on relations between East and West.

THE SACRED HEAD

LEAVING THIS ASIDE for the moment, it has also been suggested that the Templars may have been the guardians of a relic of such importance that it even outshone the Grail – though in fact the two were connected. According to arguments put forward by Ian Wilson and, more recently, Noel Currer-Briggs, both of whom offer considerable documentation, there is every reason to believe that the object known as the Mandylion passed through the hands of the order during the height of its power, and that this same object, which seems to have been a piece of cloth, folded several times and stretched between frames of wood, may have been the shroud of Christ, apparently lost to the world during the siege of Constantinople in 1204, but possibly disguised in this form to prevent it falling into Muslim hands.

This same relic is nowadays to be found in the Cathedral of Turin, and is the subject of continuing controversy and world-wide scientific investigation.

Thomas Hardy's vision of Tintagel as the seat of King Mark, long believed to be Arthur's birthplace; drawn from memory, 1923, as the frontispiece of his *The Famous Tragedy of the Queen of Cornwall*

If Wilson and Currer-Briggs are right, and there is no reason why they should not be, then not only does this present the Templars as possessing a sacred relic but it also goes some way towards explaining another of the 'blasphemies' of which they were accused.

This concerned the worship of a graven idle called Baphomet (usually accepted as a corruption of Muhammad) and described as a bearded head wearing a crown. This could easily be a garbled understanding of the Mandylion, which was folded so that only the bearded face of Christ, marked with the wounds caused by the Crown of Thorns, could be seen.

In both the *Perlesvaus* and the Cistercian-inspired *Queste del Saint Graal*, which, along with the rest of the *Vulgate Cycle*, was composed at St Bernard's monastery at Clairvaux, there are echoes of this mysterious image. In *Perlesvaus* King Arthur himself witnesses the Grail Mass, and when he looks towards the altar, 'It seemed to him that the holy hermit [who was officiating] held between his hands a man bleeding from his side and in his plams and in his feet, and crowned with thorns . . . (Bryant, 1982).

In the *Queste* we find Galahad at mass in the Temple of Sarras, the Holy City of the Grail, where the vessel is kept in an Ark standing upon a silver table – an image that reflects the model of the Holy Sepulchre found in every Templar *commanderie* throughout the world, where their most sacred rites were performed.

So we have the Templars, based at the site of Solomon's Temple, guarding a sacred relic, with special devotion to the Virgin, supported by St Bernard – elements all recognizable from the traditions of the Grail. Approved by the Pope, their rule written by one of the foremost churchmen in the Western world, they became for a time the highest standard of earthly power.

The whole of Western Christendom had grown used to the idea of the knight. The Templars were super-knights, combining the skill of fighting men with the spiritual fervour of the priesthood. We should not be surprised if many of the Grail writers took the order as a model not only for the Grail chivalry but also for the Round Table.

And here also the notion that too much power carries its own built-in law of self-destruction is apparent. Might can be harnessed for right; but when there are too many wrongs to right, when the kingdom of Jerusalem had been secured, however uneasily, the Templars, like the Round Table, fell apart. Accumulations of wealth and power served only to provoke jealously and fear. The earthly Jerusalem was but a symbol of the heavenly city after all; discontent bred by heaviness of time and stale custom shook the high purpose with which the Crusaders had set forth. In consolidating an earthly kingdom, they had lost sight of the heavenly one. A scapegoat was required and the Templars provided it.

So, by a supreme irony, the warriors of God, whose order had been founded to uphold the highest ideals of Christendom, as well as of knighthood, were accused of denying God, defaming the Cross, worshipping false idols and practising unnatural vices.

Joseph of Arimathea sets sail for Britain by Horace Knowles. Joseph is believed to have brought the cup of the last supper to Britain, and so begun the legend of the Grail in this land

The Hero Sets Sail by Huszti Horvath

They were wiped out with total and ruthless brutality (though some survived in Scotland); but their memory lingered, through the Grail romances, written by Cistercian monks who perhaps knew full well the identity of the Grail Family.

THE KINGS OF THE GRAIL

THE TEMPLE OF THE GRAIL, wherever it stood, whether in the realm of fancy or of fact, was established in the minds and hearts of medieval Grail seekers. Whoever its true guardians were, they continued to carry out their appointed task – as they surely continue to do today. Of those whose names rise to the surface from the mists which surround the inner tradition of the Grail, certain figures stand out. We might name Melchizadek, the priest-king of Salem, who in biblical tradition made the first offering of bread and wine long before the Eucharist was celebrated. Solomon himself, master of wisdom, seems to have held the cup, or at least the symbolic power it contains, for a time, and to have passed it on to others of his line. Even Jesus, who prayed that the cup of his agony might pass from him, may be in some senses a Grail guardian. While Joseph of Arimathea, and the line he founded, carried the mystery into the age of Arthur and beyond. Perceval's parti-coloured half-brother Feirefitz, wedded to the Grail princess Repanse de Schuoy, begot on her a son who was named Lohengrin, and he in turn sired an even greater figure of mystery and might: Prester John.

The first mention of this character, little more than a rumour, comes in a medieval chronicle which, for the year 1145, relates that a certain Bishop Hugh of Cabalah visited Rome and was told how, some years before:

. . . a certain Priest and King named John, who lives on the further side of Persia and Armenia, in the remote East, and who with all his people were Christians . . . had overcome the royal brothers *Samiardi*, Kings of the Medes and Persians, and had captured Eckbattana, their capital and residence. . . . The said John advanced to the help of the Church of Jerusalem; but when he had reached the river [Tygris] he had not been able to take his army across the river in any vessel. He had then turned North, where he had learned that it was all frozen by the winter cold. He had lingered there for some time, waiting for the frost, but because of the wild weather . . . [was] forced to return home after losing much of his army because of the unaccustomed climate.

(Slessarev)

Chalice of the Abbot Suger of St Denis: one of several cups believed to be the Grail

What is the truth behind this extraordinary account? We have to remember that at the time the threat of invasion from the East hung over the West rather like that of atomic war in the twentieth century. The perilously slender hold of the Crusaders over the kingdom of Jerusalem was constantly in danger of failing, with a consequent inrush of Muslim armies expected to follow. News of a crushing defeat 'in the remote East' was a morale-booster comparable to hearing that Hitler's forces had been turned back by the Russians during the last war. Thus we must admit at once that there is a strong element of wish-fulfilment behind the various references to a Christian king in the East.

Be that as it may, in 1165 there appeared a mysterious letter, copies of which found their way to Pope Alexander III, the King of France, the Emperor in Constantinople (Manuel Commenius) and the Holy Roman Emperor Frederick II – that is, the spiritual and temporal rulers of Western Christendom. The letter purported to come from no lesser person than Prester John himself, and it is a most intriguing document.

It begins:

Prester John, by the Grace of God most powerful king over all Christian kings, greetings to the Emperor of Rome and the King of France, our friends. We wish you to learn about us, our position, the government of our land, our people and our beasts. . . . We attest and inform you by our letter, sealed with our seal, of the condition and character of our land and men. And if you desire . . . to come hither to our country, we shall make you on account of your good reputation our successors and we shall grant you vast lands, manors, and mansions.

(Slessarev)

The letter continues in this style for some twenty pages, describing a land overflowing with goodness and riches, ruled over by the benign Priest-King, whose crown is the 'highest . . . on earth', and whose sway

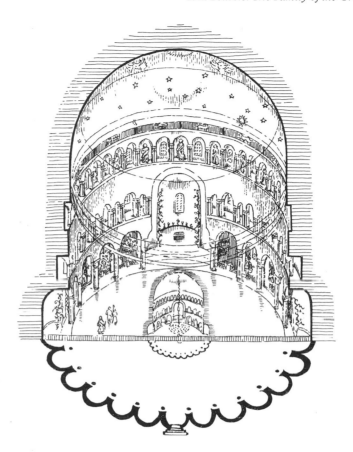

A thirteenth-century plan of a proposed, but never constructed, Temple of the Grail (after Lars Ringbom)

extends over forty-two other Christian kings. The writer then goes on: 'Between us and the Saracens there flows a river called Ydonis which comes from the terrestrial paradise and is full of precious stones . . . and of each we know its name and its magical power.'

Finally he exhorts the rulers of Christendom to put to death 'those treacherous Templars and pagans' and concludes 'in the year five hundred and seven since the year of our birth'.

The letter is a forgery. Of this there can be no doubt. The style, as well as the contents, clearly derive from identifiable, mostly Eastern sources – an ironic fact when we consider that Prester John was set up as a bitter foe of the Muslims! What we have here is a description of a semi-attainable, paradisaical place filled with wonders, offering spiritual as well as temporal pleasures – rather like the country of the Grail, in fact, as much of the text bears out. Indeed, we should hardly be surprised to find the extraordinary Temple of the Grail from Albrecht von Scharfenburg's poem appear in this setting. Both are the product of the same impulse, the desire to return to our home, the earthly paradise from which Adam and Eve were driven forth.

Prester John, as here presented, is a recognizable archetype, belonging to the race known as 'Withdrawn Kings', once great and noble beings who have withdrawn to an inner plane of existence, from which they watch over the progress of humanity and occasionally take a direct hand in historical events. Merlin is another such, as are Melchizedek, the biblical Enoch, King Arthur and the angelic Sandalphon. John, whose title means simply 'Priest-King', is the product of several vague historical personages, half-remembered accounts of Alexander the Great, various kings of Ethiopia and more than one Tartar lord.

But he is something more than this. Whether Wolfram found a reference to Prester John as the offspring of the Grail knights or made up the connection, he touched upon a deep vein. John represented all that was best in Christendom. He suffered none of the traits of corruption or heresy which hung over much of the West like a dark cloud. He was all-powerful and all-good, and he was the guardian of a great secret – the Holy Grail.

THE LINEAGE OF THE GRAIL

THE DESCENT of the Grail lineage is thus a metaphysical one. It includes mystics, seekers after truth, alchemists, magicians, kings and many more. Whatever its provenance, the Grail remains a symbol of man's desire for union with God, the return from exile on earth to a home in paradise.

Certain individuals are assigned to this task of restoration – some with a specific duty and goal in mind, others with no clue to their errand but sharing in the Family of the Grail. They make up what we might term the tribe of the Grail – a tribe drawn from no earthly lineage, with no specific racial descent; a tribe which has no territorial boundaries, no common basis for belief other than the symbol which reunites all opposites – the Grail itself.

THE TRANSATLANTIC GRAIL

AMONG THE NAMED INDIVIDUALS who have guarded the Grail, one has recently come to light whose life adds a significant chapter to the Grail's inner history. This is Prince Henry Sinclair (or St Clair), Earl of the Orkney Islands, who lived from 1345 to 1400 and is said to have made a transatlantic voyage around 1398, some ninety years before Christopher Columbus. Two recent books have set out this possible scenario: *The Holy Grail Across the Atlantic* by Michael Bradley, and *The Sword and the Grail* by Andrew Sinclair, who is a direct descendant of Prince Henry.

Both tell a similar story, though the latter has a more firm grounding in historical fact. Essentially, they detail Sinclair's voyage across the Atlantic

to what is now known as Nova Scotia. There he established a settlement near Pictou in present-day Canada, where some speculative ruins can still be seen.

This much is more or less historically verifiable – though most of the evidence comes from a suspect manuscript known as *The Zeno Narrative*, in which two Venetian sailors describe the voyage they made, under the leadership of Sinclair, to several curiously named lands, including Estotiland, Drogio and Norumbega.

What makes all this of interest in the context of the present book is that, according to both the above-named writers, Sinclair's voyage was paid for by the Templars and he might well have taken the teachings of the Grail with him, in the hope of establishing a safe haven away from the persecutions of the Grail-inspired Templar and Cathar fraternities. If this is true – and there is certainly a good deal of evidence to support it – then the Grail mysteries may have found a secure base in Canada and North America, where Sinclair later seems to have settled briefly in the area of present-day Massachusetts.

The connection with the St Clairs is certainly interesting. The family is widely known to have had links with both the Templars and later the Freemasons, while their home, at Rosslyn in Scotland, has its own intriguing associations with the Grail story. Rosslyn Chapel, built in the fifteenth century to designs drawn up by the 3rd Earl, William St Clair, is an extraordinary compendium of mystical symbolism and reference to ancient traditions. Around its walls and ceiling are to be found references to Norse, Celtic, Templar and Masonic traditions, the Green Man, the Grail and others as yet undefined. On the grave of William de St Clair is a possible representation of the Grail. Then there is the so-called 'Prentice Pillar'. This unique and beautifully carved pillar probably represents the Norse Tree of Life, Yggdrasil, and the story is told that when the master mason who carved it was away in Rome, his apprentice completed the work even more spectacularly than his master. He, on returning home, was so enraged that he killed the apprentice. A carving of a man with a head wound is said to commemorate this. But aside from this story, there is also a persistent tradition that a cup, said to be the Grail itself, is somehow enclosed within the pillar. Whatever the truth of this, it makes for interesting speculation.

If Prince Henry Sinclair did take the Grail, or its teachings, to the New World in 1398, it is equally possible that one of his descendants brought it back to Scotland in the fifteenth century and hid it in the pillar. Certainly the very definite survival of the Templars in that part of the country, and the subsequent rise of Scottish Freemasonry, all seem to point to a focus of interest in and around the area of Rosslyn.

It may well be that the truth will never be known, and that it is, anyway, futile to look for a physical Grail, but the passage of years has only added to the mystery which surrounds this sacred object, and evidence of its guardians serves to keep the ideas it represents to the forefront of contemporary seekers.

The Santo Milagro: a chalice and reliquaries from twelfth-century Spain sometimes identified with the Grail

THE SECRET QUEST

IF THE GRAIL had its guardians it also had its enemies, those who sought to wield its power for their own ends. One of the most bizarre stories of this kind concerns the attempt by the Nazies – in particular Heinrich Himmler – to discover the whereabouts of the Grail and so win the Second World War.

The Family of the Grail by an unknown Renaissance artist

This strange Grail quest was led by a German scholar named Otto Rahn, author of the book *Kreuzzug gegen den Graal* (*Crusade Against the Grail*) published in Freiburg in 1933. This book examined a little-known theory that the Cathars had somehow come into possession of the Grail and had hidden it in a vast network of caves below the sacred mountain of Munsalvache, one of the main strongholds of the Cathars and the last of their fortresses to fall in the Albigensian Crusade of 1208. So strong was the belief in this idea that when, during the long siege of Montsegur, the commander of the Cathar forces appeared in the battlements dressed in silver armour, the besieging army temporarily fled, convinced that 'the Grail Knight' had come to defend his fellows. Rahn believes that the Grail quest was a Cathar allegory which hid the true essence of their secret teachings. Wolfram's text, or rather the original writings of the mysterious Kyot of Provence (the centre of Cathar activity) was seen as an elaborately disguised rendition of the Cathar initiation ritual. Rahn also believed – despite strong evidence to the contrary – that the Grail was a physical object, and that it had been smuggled out of Montsegur the night before the castle fell, and had been hidden by the last of the Cathars.

This prompted Himmler, the head of Hitler's secret police, who had based the SS on the great Arthurian chivalric order, to send a team of crack troops, under the nominal leadership of Obersturmführer (Leutnant) Rahn, to seek the hidden Grail and carry it back to Nazi Germany.

Thankfully this search was unsuccessful (who would wish to speculate on the possible outcome if the Nazis had recovered the Grail?) and Rahn's claims were generally discredited.

THE ENDLESS QUEST

BUT THE SEARCH for the Grail does not end there. Its story continues to exert an extraordinary and powerful influence over many people who are drawn to seek it in many different ways and by many different paths to this very day. Mysteries surrounding events such as Henry Sinclair's voyage, the fall of the Templars, the persecution of the gentle and peace-loving Albigensians, the Nazi obsession with the Grail, and the continued investigation of people, places and things which have been connected to the Grail serve only to keep its secrets ever more deeply hidden. While there are those who would like to see this holy relic in a museum case behind glass walls, it continues to elude all such treasure seekers, and to blaze its own fiery and incandescent trail across the skies. Like the comet stated by Merlin to be the announcement of Arthur's coming, or the vessel which floated through the hall of Camelot and began the great Arthurian quest, the Grail continues to be a beacon to all who believe in the importance of a spiritual quest. Arthur and the Round Table Fellowship who went in search of this wondrous thing are not forgotten as long as there are those who continue the quest in their own time.

We need only to look at the example of the two young knights mentioned in *Perlesvaus* who, having heard the stories of the quest, long after the passing of Arthur and his heroes, visited the Chapel of the Grail – then in ruins – and remained there for a long while. At length they went out into the world again and were perceived to be changed. But whenever they were asked what had occurred to bring about this change, they would answer only: 'Go where we went and you will see.' The same is true to this day, and those who seek out Arthur and the Grail are still part of the ongoing quest, their own experience adding to the tradition even as I write, or you read, these words.

The Falling

THE FOLLOWING STORY is inspired by two very different sources. The first is the suggestion, embedded in Wolfram von Eschenbach's Parzival *and elsewhere, that the Grail was a stone from the crown of the angel of light, Lucifer, which fell to earth during a struggle between angels of light and darkness which shook the very foundations of heaven. The other is a fragmentary gnostic story which describes the fall of Lucifer into matter and his battle with the apocalyptic Beast, whose place in the heart of the world he takes.*

◆ ◆ ◆

H E HUNG ON THE EDGE of the sky like a tear in the eye of a queen. Then he fell and the darkness enclosed him, wrapping him round in its sticky web. Only the bright glow of his sword, held out before him like a torch, illumined his path. The path that was no path, the direction that was without direction, the goal that was unknown to him because he has not been given any chance to consider it.

Words had been expunged from his mind, so that he no longer possessed the language to formulate speech. Only a last brief glimpse of the Sword of Flame seared his brain, and the sense of the Shaper's thoughts rang in his mind. 'You are no longer my Son. You have betrayed me. There is no place here for you!'

Then there was only the falling, the darkness, and a silence which was made worse because somewhere, like a distant echo, he heard singing – knew it was singing even though he had no words for it – and longed to join his own voice to that of the Others.

But he neither knew nor could remember who those Others were, who the Shaper was, and why he could still see, like a last echoing cry, a flash of red wings. . . .

His own were white, shading to gold. He knew this even though he could see nothing in the darkness. Nor could he turn his head. His eyes seemed fixed, looking forward at the green glitter of his sword.

Gradually, so gradually that at first it was no more than a vague sensation in the deepest recesses of his mind, he became aware of a change in the texture of the darkness. In some way, though he groped for the concepts to fashion the thought, somehow the darkness was growing thicker. His descent began, imperceptibly at first, to slow.

And then ahead, giving for the first time dimension to his fall, he espied something else, something that was not himself nor his sword – a dim, distant break in the darkness, as though someone had thrust a pin through the vast velvet drape and let in some light – always supposing there was light, somewhere beyond the endless-seeming dark.

Slowly the dim glint took on shape and substance. A tiny whirling ball of light and shadow, intricately patterned with spirals of what, in some fashion, he knew to be earth and water.

The ball lay before him, captured in an eddy of time and space into which he fell like a stone into a pool. The noise of his landing must have woken the heavens themselves, but raised no echoes here. Its effect upon him was, however, vast. He found that he could hear.

Sounds filled his head and with them came words that gave them substance. He stood upon something he knew to be 'sand', saw 'waves' strike a 'shore', felt a thousand glimmering droplets touch his face – 'rain' something within him said.

His other senses followed in quick succession. Smell came first, and with it a tang of salt air and a scent he associated at once with greenness and growth. In his ears rang the sound of the waves hammering at the sandy shoreline. His fingers suddenly relaxed around the hilt of his sword, as the sensation of touch returned and he realized that he was still gripping the weapon as though everything depended upon it.

He looked at the bright blade and saw the green flame still lit within its faceted and polished surfaces. Its use fascinated him. It had seemed no more than a beacon, but now he knew it for a weapon which could be used for a purpose he did not yet understand.

Reflexively, he arched his wings and felt the play of the wind within them. He looked up at the sky and found its blueness pleasing. A bright bead of light shone down upon him and he stretched out his hands to touch it – only to find that it was too far. A sadness overtook him them, a sense of loss.

He stood thus for a long time, while the bright bead of light fell down

the sky (fell, like himself?) and turned slowly to crimson. At his feet the sea turned first purple then to the colour of milk. He raised his eyes and saw another globe of light hanging where the other had been. This was closer, imbued with a milky-white sheen. Again he reached towards it and again it was beyond his touch.

Then, as he looked with longing and sorrow towards the light, something came between it and himself. A shadow, shapeless and formless at first, but slowly taking shape. Winged, like himself, but different . . . a long neck and a hideous head – somehow he knew that he was beautiful and that it, whatever it was, was dark and misshapen where he was light and formed to the Shaper's will.

With this thought came the notion of his own ability. The sword rose in his hands and the green flame leapt within it as though at his unspoken command. The Shadow spied it and turned upon him such a concentrated beam of malevolence that it was as though a breath of fire had struck at him. Almost, he staggered. But then an answering strength awoke within him, and he sent forth a ray of light from his open hand which broke upon the Shadow's front and sent it roiling backwards upon itself. . . .

But only for a moment. The Beast uncoiled its vast length and struck down with a speed impossible to its size. A lash of pure hate and fear struck him and pain awoke within him. So new was the sensation that he scarcely felt it at first. But anger awoke then, and strength, and knowledge of a deeper kind than before, and he knew that here was purpose, where before there had been only emptiness.

Without thought he drew back the hand in which his sword was grasped and flung it forward and up at the shadow above him. Trailing a tail of green fire it flashed through the darkness and struck deep within the heart of the Beast. A terrible soundless cry echoed across the face of the sky and the ground beneath his feet trembled and seemed itself to cry out. The Beast spun away into blackness, its terrible body ruptured and hurt beyond healing.

There was a moment of stillness that brought back to his mind the silence of his long fall, then the ground shook again and a fissure opened beneath his feet. As he fell – again, falling! – he caught a final glimpse of the sword. It had passed through the Beast, or perhaps been disgorged by it. Now it arced across the sky like a comet, trailing green fire. Then it was gone from his sight and the rushing darkness and warmth of the earth sur-

The Falling

rounded him in a fast embrace. Somewhere he became aware of a voice which spoke out of the darkness.

'Come. Sleep. Be at one with Me. Let us dream together.'

And at once he knew peace, such peace as he had never thought to know again. After millennia of wakefulness he could sleep at last. And dream.

And in his dream he saw again where the sword flashed in the heavens, curving upward until it could go no further, then beginning to fall back towards the place where he had stood in contemplation of a new world, a world of which he was now a part. As it fell, the sword began to change. The texture of the air through which it fell bent it in upon itself. The point was driven back within itself, and the hilt curved outward to form an enclosing rim. Finally, it had a new shape entirely – that of a green cup-shaped vessel, from which something of the green light of its former master still shone – though dimmer now. It came to rest at last, on a table of stone, a vast flat-topped mountain which rose out of the warm lands like a fist. There it rested and there, for a time, he lost sight of it.

Thus began his dream, which was to encompass long ages. Many things there were to see in that time – the coming of men, and a growing knowledge of good and evil, light and dark. Sometimes he was able to speak to one or another of them, and heard his name – a name he had never answered to before – cursed for the knowledge he offered. And at last, after ages of darkness, he saw the cup which had been formed from his sword taken up and wielded by hands other than his own. Then the cup was lost, and he saw men set forth in search of it, following a last subtle gleam of the old light – no longer green, but silvered now, like the colour of old bone. He knew that one day it would be found again, and that while the search continued it would not be forgotten. This gave him some comfort as he lay, between waking and sleeping, in the arms of the earth, listening always for the voices of the Others whose song he would one day join.

Appendix: The Major Arthurian Texts of the Middle Ages

The following list contains a selection of the major medieval texts relating to the Arthurian legends and the story of the Grail in more or less date order. All dates are, however, strictly approximate within fifty years either side.

De Excidio et Conquestu Britanniae, Gildas   (540)
Historia Britonum, Nennius   (ninth century)
Spoils of Annwn   (tenth century)
Culhwch and Olwen   (eleventh century)
Historia Regum Britanniae, Geoffrey of Monmouth   (1136)
Erec and Enide, Chrétien de Troyes   (1169)
Lancelot, Chrétien de Troyes   (1175)
Ywain, Chrétien de Troyes   (1180)
Perceval, Chrétien de Troyes   (1185)
Roman de Brut, Wace   (1190)
First continuation of *Perceval*   (1190)
Joseph of Arimathea, Robert de Borron   (1200)
Perlesvaus   (1208)
Prose (Didot) *Perceval*   (1210)
Parzifal, Wolfram von Eschenbach   (1210)
Vulgate Cycle   (1215–35)
Second continuation of *Perceval*   (1220)
Third continuation of *Perceval*   (1220)
Diu Crone, Heinrich von dem Turlin   (1230)
Peredur   (1240)
Prose *Tristan*   (1255)
Der Jungere Titurel, Albrecht von Scharfenburg   (1274)
Perceforest   (1335)
Sone de Nansai   (1350)
Alliterative *Morte Arthure*   (1390)
Stanzaic *Le Morte Arthur*   (1400)
Sir Gawain and the Green Knight   (1420)
Morte D'Arthur, Sir Thomas Malory   (1470)

Bibliography

Angebert, Jean-Michel, *The Occult and the Third Reich*, New York, Macmillan, 1974

Bede, *A History of the English Church and People*, Harmondsworth, Penguin Books, 1955

Bernard of Clairvaux, *Treatise in Praise of the New Order of Knighthood*, New Jersey, Cistercian Publishing, 1976

Birks, Walter and R. A. Gilbert, *The Treasure of Montsegur*, London, Crucible, 1987

Bradley, Michael (with Deanna Theilman-Bean), *The Holy Grail Across the Atlantic*, Toronto, Hounslow Press, 1989

Brengle, Richard L. (ed.), *Arthur King of Britain*, New Jersey, Prentice-Hall, 1964

Bromwich, Rachel, *Triodd Ynys Prydein (The Welsh Triads)*, Cardiff, University of Wales Press, 1977

Bromwich, Rachel, A. O. H. Jarman and B. F. Roberts (eds.), *The Arthur of the Welsh*, Cardiff, University of Wales Press, 1993

Bryant, Nigel, *The High Book of the Grail: A Translation of the 13th Century Romance of Perlesvaus*, Cambridge, D. S. Brewer; Totowa, New Jersey, Rowman & Littlefield, 1978

Campbell, David E., *The Tale of Balain from the Romance of the Grail*, Evanston, Northwestern University Press, 1972

Chadwick, Nora K., *The Celtic Realms*, Harmondsworth, Penguin Books, 1967

Chrétien de Troyes, *Arthurian Romances*, translated by William W. Kibler and Carleton W. Carroll, Harmondsworth, Penguin Books, 1991 (*Erec, Cliges, The Knight of the Cart, The Knight with the Lion, The Story of the Grail*)

– *Perceval, or The Story of the Grail*, translated by Nigel Bryant, Cambridge, D. S. Brewer, 1982

Collingwood, R. G. and J. N. L. Myres, *Roman Britain and the English Settlements*, Oxford University Press, 1936

Comfort, William W., *The Quest of the Holy Grail*, London, J. M. Dent, 1926

Coughlan, Ronan, *The Illustrated Encyclopedia of the Arthurian Legends*, Shaftesbury, Element Books, 1993

Currer-Briggs, Noel, *The Shroud and the Grail*, London, Weidenfeld & Nicolson, 1987

Dillon, Miles, *The Cycles of the Kings*, London, J. M. Dent, 1946 (includes *Baille in Scaile*)

Evans, Sebastian, *In Quest of the Holy Graal*, London, J. M. Dent, 1898

Geoffrey of Monmouth, *History of the Kings of Britain*, translated by Lewis Thorp, Harmondsworth, Penguin Books, 1966

Giles, J. A. (ed.), *Six Old English Chronicles*, London, G. Bell & Sons, 1910 (Nennius, Gildas, Geoffrey of Monmouth)

Goodrich, N. L., *The Ways of Love*, USA, Beacon Press, 1964 (includes Robert de Borron)

Guest, Charlotte, *The Mabinogion*, London, J. M. Dent, 1906

Jarman, A. O. H., *Geoffrey of Monmouth*, Cardiff, University of Wales Press, 1966

Jones, Thomas, 'The Black Book of Carmarthen Stanzas of the Graves', *Proceedings of the British Academy*, 53 (1967), pp. 97–137

Jung, Emma and Marie-Louise von Franz, *The Grail Legend*, London, Hodder & Stoughton, 1971

Lacey, Norris J. and Geoffrey Ashe, *The Arthurian Handbook*, New York, Garland Press, 1988

Layamon, in *Arthurian Chronicles*, translated by E. Mason, London, J. M. Dent, 1962

Loomis, R. S., *The Grail from Celtic Myth to Christian Symbol*, Cardiff, University of Wales Press, 1963

Malory, Sir Thomas, *Morte D'Arthur*, New York, University Books, 1961

Markale, Jean, *King Arthur King of Kings*, London, Gordon & Cremonesi, 1977

Matarasso, P. M. (trans.), *The Quest for the Holy Grail*, Harmondsworth, Penguin Books, 1969

Matthews, Caitlín, *Mabon and the Mysteries of Britain: An Exploration of the Mabinogion*, London, Arkana, 1987

– *Arthur and the Sovereignty of Britain: King and Goddess in the Mabinogion*, London, Arkana, 1989a

– *The Elements of Celtic Tradition*, Shaftesbury, Element Books, 1989b

– *The Elements of the Goddess*, Shaftesbury, Element Books, 1989c

– *The Arthurian Tarot: A Hallowquest Pack and Handbook* (with John Matthews), London, Aquarian Press, 1990

– *The Celtic Book of the Dead*, London, Thorsons, 1992

Matthews, John, *The Grail Seeker's Companion* (with Marian Green), Wellingborough, Aquarian Press, 1986

– *At the Table of the Grail*, London, Arkana, 1987a

– *Warriors of Arthur* (with Bob Stewart), Poole, Blandford Press, 1987b

– *The Aquarian Guide to British and Irish Mythology* (with Caitlín Matthews), Aquarian Press, Wellingborough, 1988a

– *An Arthurian Reader*, Aquarian Press, Wellingborough, 1988b

– *Celtic Battle Heroes* (with Bob Stewart), Poole, Firebird Books, 1988c

– *Fionn mac Cumhail: Champion of Ireland*, Poole, Firebird Books, 1988d

– *Elements of Arthurian Tradition*, Shaftesbury, Element Books, 1989a

– *Legendary Britain: An Illustrated Journey* (with R. J. Stewart), London, Cassell, 1989b

– *The Arthurian Book of Days*, London, Sidgewick & Jackson; New York, St Martin's Press, 1990a

– *A Celtic Reader*, Wellingborough, Aquarian Press, 1990b

– *Elements of the Grail Tradition*, Shaftesbury, Element Books, 1990c

– *Gawain, Knight of the Goddess*, Wellingborough, Aquarian Press, 1990d

– *The Grail: Quest for the Eternal*, London, Thames & Hudson, 1981; New York, Crossroads, 1990e

– *Hallowquest: Tarot Magic and the Arthurian Mysteries* (with Caitlín Matthews), Wellingborough, Aquarian Press, 1990f

– *Household of the Grail*, Wellingborough, Aquarian Press, 1990g

– *Taliesin: Shamanism and the Bardic Mysteries in Britain and Ireland* (with additional material by Caitlín Matthews), London, Harper Collins, 1990h

– *A Glastonbury Reader*, Wellingborough, Aquarian Press, 1991

– *Ladies of the Lake* (with Caitlín Matthews), Wellingborough, Aquarian Press, 1992

– *From the Isles of Dream*, Floris Books/Lindisfarne Press, 1993a

– *Little Book of Celtic Wisdom* (with Caitlín Matthews), Shaftesbury, Element Books, 1993b

Meeks, John and Doris, 'The Temple of the Grail', in *The Golden Blade*, Rudolf Steiner Press, 1981

Morris, John, *The Age of Arthur*, London, Weidenfeld & Nicolson, 1973

– *British History and the Welsh Annals*, London and Chichester, Phillimore, 1980 (Nennius and the *Annales Cambriae*)

Parry, J. J., *The Vita Merlini*, Illinois: University of Illinois, 1925

Roach, William, *The Continuations of the Old French Perceval*, Philadelphia, American Philosophical Society, 1949–52 (3 vols.)

Schlauch, Margaret, *Medieval Narrative: A Book of Translations*, New York, Gordian Press, 1969

Sinclair, Andrew, *The Sword and the Grail*, New York, Crown Publishing, 1993

Skeels, Dell, *The Romance of Perceval in Prose: A Translation of the Didot Perceval*, Washington, University of Washington Press, 1966

Slessarev, V., *Prester John: The Letter and the Legend*, Minneapolis, University of Minnesota, 1959

Sommer, H. Oskar, *The Vulgate Version of the Arthurian Romances*, Washington, The Carnegie Institute 1908–16 (8 vols.)

Stein, Walter Johannes, *The Ninth Century: World History in the Light of the Holy Grail* (with an introduction by John Matthews), London, Temple Lodge Press, 1991

Thompson, A. W., *The Elucidation*, New York, Institute of French Studies, 1931

Tolstoy, Nikolai, 'Nennius, Chapter 56', *Bulletin of Celtic Studies*, vol. 19, 1961, pp. 118–62

Wace, Robert, *The Brut*, translated by E. Mason, London, J. M. Dent, 1962

Wheeler, Francis Rolt, *Mystic Gleams from the Holy Grail*, London, Rider & Co., n.d. [1948]

Williams, Hugh, *Two Lives of Gildas by the Monk of Ruys and Caradoc of Llancarven*, Llanerch Enterprises, 1990

Wilson, Ian, *The Turin Shroud*, London, Gollancz, 1979

Wolfram von Eschenbach, *Parzival*, translated by A. T. Hatto, Harmondsworth, Penguin Books, 1980

– *Titurel*, translated by Charles E. Passage, New York, Frederick Ungar, 1984

Index